GET YOUR

GREATER

GET YOUR

GREATER

The True Story of How One Man Went from
Being a Homeless Single Father on the Streets
of DC to Finding His Greatness

MARK SHEPARD

BMcTALKS Press
4980 South Alma School Road
Suite 2-493
Chandler, Arizona 85248

Volume pricing is available to bulk orders placed by corporations, associations, and others. For bulk order details and for media inquiries, please contact Press 49 at info@press49.com or 833.PRESS49 (833.773.7749).

FIRST EDITION

Library of Congress Control Number: 2023901915

ISBN: 978-1-953315-27-4

BIOGRAPHY & AUTOBIOGRAPHY/Personal Memoirs
SELF-HELP/Spiritual

Interior design by Medlar Publishing Solutions Pvt Ltd., India.
Cover design by Press 49.

Printed in the United States of America.

Table of Contents

Preface .... *vii*

Introduction .... *ix*

CHAPTER 1   The Rough Beginning 1

CHAPTER 2   The Day I Thought My Heart
             Would Burst... 15

CHAPTER 3   The Meeting.. 27

CHAPTER 4   A Turning Point....................................... 41

CHAPTER 5   The New Beginning 49

CHAPTER 6   What Lies Ahead...................................... 61

CHAPTER 7   The Encounter 75

CHAPTER 8   The Transformation.................................. 83

CHAPTER 9   Refused and Limited................................ 95

CHAPTER 10   The Weight Removed 111

CHAPTER 11   The Gift 121

CHAPTER 12   The Journey Continues............................. 133

Epilogue: They Saved My Life *145*

Author's Note *147*

Getting to Your Greater Reflection Questions *149*

Preface

Get Your Greater is a true story of how I went from being a homeless single father on the streets of DC to getting my life together. I found that through each stage of my life, there were golden opportunities presented to me in the most unusual ways—even when no one would help me, even when people who were close to me and who knew I was down but didn't bother to lend a hand—these were still valuable jewels that strengthened me as a father, a friend, and a man.

Please understand that by no means is this book a shot at the persons involved in my life's journey. In fact, I thank each and every one of them. I know that it was God's plan that I was able to go from being homeless and, at times, having to sleep on a grate to be great. And I know you can do the same—that you can get to a place where you are even greater than you are now.

Everyone's life is filled with ups and downs, and sometimes it feels like the downs far outweigh the ups. We can be at our lowest today, and in the very next moment, we can be the happiest we've ever been. Most of those events are split-second flashes that we never saw coming, but we must always be aware, plugged-in, and alive. It's in the most difficult of times when we learn the greatest lessons. It is moments like these that define us in the end. When you are in the midst of going through it, it's hard to see the lessons or the silver linings; and as a result, many miss out on those opportunities, finding it almost impossible to regain a solid footing. I get it. Being down and in a state of not having can be frustrating. Very frustrating. Trust me. I know. But I also know you can get up. You can get going. You can get your greater.

Please use this book to find inspiration to follow your dreams. Delay is not denial. The problems you face today are not signs of the end. It's not. You must and will surely reach your goals, and you, too, will be able to inspire others to find their footing and regain life's purpose. There is greatness in you, and you only have to know it, believe it, live it, and go get it.

Introduction

From 2008 until 2013, I was homeless with nothing and no one to help me. No family, no friends—I was just out! The obvious question is why didn't my family help me? Or what about friends? Why didn't I turn to any of them?

When it comes to my family, I can't give a definitive reason for why I didn't go to them. It has always been a difficult relationship where I have been the constant outsider in the family, so I didn't necessarily feel comfortable going to them. And as for my friends, I had burned so many bridges with my mean and disrespectful attitude, so in retrospect, and to tell you the truth, I wouldn't have wanted to be around me either. I didn't know how to reach out for help—what words to use and how to say them, and this was all because of the deep hurt and pain inside of me that stemmed from my childhood.

Please understand the real friends who wanted to help simply were not in positions to help, and that is because if they had done so, they would have placed more stress and strain on themselves and their immediate families with trying to help me. Those friends had already taken in other family members to live with them, or their place was too small to accommodate me, or they just lived too far away in other states. But they really wanted to help, and I get it!

However, I was out in the cold world with no money, no food, and no safe place to lay my head. And how I got there was because I was broken—I was damaged goods. I was mean, disrespectful, abusive, and lost. I did not know love, but I wanted love. And when it came, I destroyed it. I turned good people against me. I did to others what had been done to me. I had no control of my emotions, and for the most part, by being a grown man, I was too ashamed to ask for help. How do you ask for help as a man when, as a man, you are supposed to have all the answers?

With years of hurt balled up in me, the least little thing would send me in any direction coupled with anger or sadness. So, I became homeless, and it was all my fault—what happened leading up to my homelessness and everything that happened thereafter. It was all my fault, and this is the story of how it all unfolded—my *true* story.

I was really living a day-to-day life that was so hard, and I felt so lost and broken—I had many days of feeling thrown away and less than crap. But later, I learned that I was set apart by God, and I didn't know why. Let alone did I see that it was He who was putting me on a new path to greatness.

CHAPTER 1

The Rough Beginning

"I'm fucking him, and I don't plan to stop!"

It was those nine maddening, blinding words that sent my world tumbling.

I should have seen this coming, though. I should have known it was inevitable that things would take a turn for the worse. You see, everything came to a head when I married my second wife, Kim, and I was deep in what I thought was love.

I went about life with blinders on, unaware of the trouble that was brewing in the center of me. I realized that I was being overlooked in a lot of family affairs, which, as the man of the house, was extremely unsettling. I was always the last to know everything. If my wife was sick, I was the last to know. If she needed anything, I was the last to know. I was an outsider in my own home.

When I went to her to ask her about this, to ask her why I was essentially being locked out of her life, she told me that I didn't matter, that she was going to do whatever she wanted to do regardless of how it impacted me or our marriage. Not knowing how to deal with this, I completely lost control. I cursed, then we would fight with me taking the lead, throwing her around, shaking and choking her. This is nothing whatsoever that I'm proud of nor is it anything I would even *dare* to think of doing now. It was a low moment in my life—the lowest—where I needed help, where I needed to understand how to have a healthy relationship, where I needed to know how to communicate effectively, where I needed to understand how to deal with the hurt in my *own* life before I could try to build a life with someone else. How does the saying go?—Hurt people hurt people. That's what was happening with me and all the pain from my past that I had subconsciously brought into the relationship. At the time, though, I didn't know that was what was happening.

We would fight, the fight would come to an end, a couple of days would pass, and that's when the ignoring would resume—and the non-communicative, sarcastic, disrespectful, mean wife would show back up. And I don't know which was worse—the days of fighting or the days in between when we weren't fighting because even when we weren't at odds with each other, it was still tough.

It was tough. It was scary. It was hurtful. It was lonely. It was so bad that I would feel like I was in a different world when I stepped outside our home. The cocoon of negativity behind closed doors had me wrapped in a strange feeling. I would pray, I would listen to gospel music by Fred Hammond, I would cook, I would clean, and I would try to do everything I could to make the apartment peaceful. Regardless, Kim would still leave for days at a time or if she *was* around, she wouldn't even talk to me and would simply act as if I wasn't there.

This went on for years—three long, hard years from 2005, the year before Kim and I married, until 2008. I thought that I was stupid for letting this woman treat me like this, but it's true—once again, hurt people hurt people. She was hurt by her life, and I was hurt by mine. We didn't know it at the time although we should have—we had absolutely no business being together.

I tried my best to show what I *thought* was love, caring for her all times of the night when she was sick. As she convalesced at home and during long hospital stays, I also cared for all the children—both her two girls from a previous relationship as well as the daughter and twin sons that Kim and I had together—while I also worked a full-time job.

You see, I knew how to tend to the day-to-day obligations that automatically came with being the head of the household; I knew how to take care of the obvious, what was right there in my face—lend a caring hand to an ailing wife, provide the basic needs to children, and dutifully work a job. But I didn't know how to do the rest—how to love, control my emotions, listen, and agree to disagree—and man, it was bad.

My wife told me that she would never love me, for me to take some time to get myself together and create a fresh start. When I say it was bad, it went so far as Kim telling me to go get myself a girlfriend!

To her credit—if I can even put it that way—she told me that she wouldn't keep my kids from me, that I would be able to see them but to just go do me. At this point, with years of being disconnected and unhappy, her perspective was as follows: If she hadn't shown me love or hadn't made love to me all this time, then why should I expect it to ever happen? Why should I expect anything to change? I should simply go do me.

Really?!

That further broke me up into so many very complex pieces—pieces that bred worry, hurt, insecurities, loneliness, and anger. But I stayed in the relationship in spite of. I'm not saying I wasn't angry or that I wasn't hurt or full of self-doubt. To the contrary, this motivated me. I tried even more although she didn't love me. I read the Word, consuming Ephesians backward and forward.

Every day, I got up early to log in to my online job as a brand marketer, then I got the two older kids up and ready for elementary school and the three older babies dressed for daycare. I made breakfast for everyone and packed Kim's lunch. Then I warmed up the van, put the babies in their car seats, and waited in the van for Kim to come downstairs. I did this every day. Patience was the leader in my life. I would hold my tongue although I was treated very badly. I wouldn't say anything, holding out hope that one day I would eventually feel love from her or hear her say something nice to me. Again, I tried even more although she didn't love me, although she didn't appreciate me, although she was seeing another man, and although she was getting advice from all the wrong people concerning our marriage.

Like I said, I was reading the Word—I really had to go to Father God on this because I didn't know what to do, where to turn, or what to say. Believe me when I say I was alone. Crying all the time for seemingly no reason made it easy for fear to set in, and in flooded all the other insecurities that caused me to question myself in everything. And still, I just couldn't find the answer—how to turn things around.

I had been begging and begging for Kim's attention for somewhere around two and a half years at this point, pleading for her to talk to me, touch me, kiss me, sit with me, stop treating me like she didn't see me. To be fair, yes, I begged, but I complained, too.

In my complaining and overall bad attitude, I was also fighting the hurt and pain inside of me, so I was fighting on two fronts. I had been abandoned before as a child, so I didn't want to be in that space again. (But hindsight is 20/20. Why should she want to talk to me, touch me, kiss me, or do anything else given I had not shown her the same love? How could I expect her to give me what I had not given her?)

Then the day came when everything changed.

I'll never forget it.

It was a cool, cloudy, rainy fall day. A Friday. I had just bought all new furniture—TVs and everything—in an effort to prove to her and her mother that I wasn't worthless. I had even gone so far as to cook dinner that day, too—fried chicken, mac and cheese, broccoli, and baked rolls—trying to win Kim's heart and demonstrate to Kim's mother and her aunts that they were wrong about me, that I really was a good man.

Kim came home from work around nine o'clock that evening, and by then, I'd already fed the children and put them to bed. But I was fighting a no-win war. That night, although I'd tried to do something nice by re-furnishing the house and making dinner for her, she took the plate of food and threw it in the trash, marched right past the new living room, and headed into our bedroom—the bedroom we still shared when she didn't decide to sleep on the couch for the night. Perplexed and feeling drained, I cleaned the kitchen then went into our bedroom where she was lying on the bed, talking on the phone.

I asked, "Can I talk to you?"

"What do you want?"

"Can you please get off the phone so we can talk? Please?!"

"No. Just say what you have to say."

Not wanting to air our business in front of whomever was on the other end but also realizing she was not going to budge, I forged ahead and asked, "Why aren't we talking anymore?"

"Well, I found someone, and I don't need you anymore."

That stung. And all the while, we had an audience, making the sting even more painful.

But she didn't stop there.

She went on to reveal she had been sleeping with the guy at her job; and as a matter of fact, he was the one who had recently paid for the kids to go to the circus, plus he was who she was on the phone with.

"I'm fucking him, and I don't plan to stop!"

A heat rapidly spread throughout my body. It started in the middle of my throat, then it expanded from there, traveling from my shoulder blades to my arms, through my elbows, wrapped around my wrists, and slithered down into my fingertips, warmly coursing throughout my body.

"Hand me the phone," I demanded.

With what seemed like an air of pride, she extended her arm to hand me her cell phone, but before I knew it, I slapped it out of her hand, sending it flying across the room. I then picked her up from where she was reclining on the bed, threw her to the other side of the bed, then swiftly walked around to meet her where she'd landed with the intent to unleash more of my rage. As I proceeded to grab her again, from the corner of my eye, I saw one of our twins, our one-year-old son, standing in the bedroom doorway. In that moment—in that flash of a moment—I came to my senses and let her go.

But it was too little too late. I had gone entirely too far. Entirely too far. I had abused her plain and simple; I was wrong, and there was no denying that. And the way it all unfolded was just as she'd hoped it would.

"You played right into my hands. I want you and the boys gone!"

But as fast as the words came out of her mouth, she changed her mind and said, "No. I want them to make your life hell."

Read: You take them. You figure it out. Do it without me.

At some point, she had called her mom who lived across the parking lot in the next building. But her mom was not at her own place, minding her own business. She was already in the hallway and had been standing outside our apartment the entire time. She promptly barged in and took my sons. Right then and there. In the middle of the night.

I had walked right into Kim's trap!

The ultimate goal had been to find a way to get rid of me, to send me into such a rage until she would have no choice but to insist I was a threat to her safety and that I needed to leave. She thought—and rightfully so—that taking my sons from me would be the ultimate infliction of pain but quickly changed course of action and thought it would be more vindictive to send me on my way to single-handedly care for our young sons. But for the time being, separating my sons from me was her ultimate revenge, to get back at me for all the hurt she'd experienced in our marriage.

I told her mom that she couldn't take my sons. She had absolutely no right to take my sons! However, her mom wasn't hearing it, and she wasn't backing down. She said that she would do everything in her power to get them permanently taken away from me. What was I to do? My hands were tied. She was intent on taking them, and I didn't want to create an even bigger scene that could have resulted in the police getting involved. It was two against one—Kim and her mom against me—so for the time being, I had to let them go.

But four days later, that Tuesday, the police *did* get involved. The sheriff served me with a restraining order, requiring me to appear in court. And once all was said and done with the court proceeding, the judge's order was I had to leave the property.

I was in total shock. I told the judge that I was the one paying the rent! I was the one paying all the utilities! I was the one paying all the bills in that apartment! How could he throw me out of my own place?! But he didn't even listen to me. While it may have all been true, none of that mattered. It wasn't about whose name was on the lease or who was paying what.

I tried to tell him what had happened and the long period of abuse I'd suffered, that I was broken and deeply hurt. And all the while, as I tried to explain myself, Kim, her mother, and her friends were sitting in the gallery, laughing at me, calling me stupid. It was so humiliating. It was like a scene in a movie, and I couldn't stop the cameras from rolling.

The judge essentially said he didn't care. The bottom line was he was adjudicating the case that was currently before him, not the past, not our emotional disconnect, not whatever may have led up to the altercation that got us to this point. In the case at hand, I was the aggressor; therefore, his ruling was I had until the end of the day to vacate the apartment. Period.

I couldn't believe it.

Feeling utterly defeated, I signed the papers and accepted my fate. But Kim didn't miss a beat. By the time I got to the apartment, the locks had already been changed, and my stuff was in the hallway along with our one-year-old twin boys, sitting in their car seats. At that point, we were homeless.

Everything that I couldn't carry with me was lost—all of my books, documents, personal effects, and all the things you simply acquire in the course of living—and Kim didn't care. But it was my fault because I didn't know how to be a man and control myself. Now, I was out in the streets, trying to find a place for the three of us.

I was met with a mix of all of the following: No one would help. No one had space. No one wanted to help.

When you're going through a tough time, that's when you find out exactly who your people are—so I accepted my reality. We slept outside, I kept them clean, and I fed them. But that didn't change the fact that we didn't have a home. We went for three weeks like this until I reached out, pleading to Kim to take them until I got on my feet, promising I would come back for them. I'm not sure if it was out of pity for me or out of love for her sons but she agreed, and I was so grateful.

As days turned into weeks and weeks turned into months, I found myself so low that I wanted to just die. But if I did that, who was going to care for my sons? I was facing a tough reality. It was so hard living on the streets without the basics to attend to hygiene. And that made finding a job nearly impossible. I'd lost my position as a brand marketer; without reliable and consistent Internet access, I was fired. I smelled like urine mixed with dirt; I had a body odor that could kill all fresh air within a six-foot radius, so without a second thought, I was turned away by every potential employer. And quite honestly, had the shoe been on the other foot, I believe I would have done the same.

Most days, I walked all night to keep from falling asleep on the open streets. Other times, I went to Union Station and slept in the stairwells, or I would stand in the depot, feigning the impression that I was a passenger, waiting on the Amtrak. I never begged for food; I most surely could have because it certainly looked easy enough to do so, and besides, the other homeless guys were doing it and eating like kings. However, I could not bring myself to be a beggar because I felt like it was stealing from families, so I went to restaurants instead and asked to wash dishes or help clean up in exchange for food or money. Some would offer the job of cleaning the restrooms, and let me tell you that in most cases, those were the nastiest places on the face of the planet. This hard labor allowed me to eat a little better, though, and have a modest amount of money. What I didn't send to the court for child support, I used to buy a toothbrush, a bar of soap, and deodorant. (I'd stopped paying the money directly to Kim because she had the courts believing I wasn't giving her any assistance for the three children she and I had together, and that simply was not true.)

I was really living a day-to-day life that was so hard, and I felt so lost and broken–I had many days of feeling thrown away and less than crap. But later, I learned that I was set apart by God, and I didn't know why. Let alone did I see that it was He who was putting me on a new path to greatness. Every day, though, I sank deeper and deeper into that dark pity party of shame, blame, lies, and no self-worth; it had become so bad that I refused to believe that God loved me, and I would just lie on the sidewalk in downtown DC and not move for days. I felt like I had no life left in me. The "What for?" attitude was ever-present, and my mindset was incredibly low so, for me, there was really nothing else to do but just give up.

Everyone I asked for help turned me down, and some of them were God-fearing, church-going people. I stood in front of different churches, asking for help to no avail. There were times when I even went inside the actual church doors and was turned away. I went looking for God and could not find Him. His people treated me worse than my enemies. Even a guy I grew up with who didn't like me gave me food; he helped me when the church wouldn't—so yea, I thought God didn't love me. But this wasn't the first time I questioned God's love for me.

What the hell?!!!!!
That's not true!
That's not how she died!
What is he saying?
And why is he
saying this?!

CHAPTER 2

The Day I Thought
My Heart Would Burst

I was happy to reach the age of thirteen. It was a milestone for me but for reasons most adolescents cannot relate to. My childhood was one of moving around a lot, living with different families that included having two people I regarded as my father for different reasons. There was my biological father, whom I refer to as "father" throughout the book, and my adoptive father whom I call "Dad."

My biological father prophesied, telling me at a young age that someone would and should kill me before I reached thirteen. He had no reasoning behind this; it was just something he said to be mean simply because that's what he did when it came to me—be mean. He'd told me he didn't want me and that I would never be his. Again, that's just what he did. So, for every birthday beyond the age of thirteen that I was blessed with, it was truly a special day.

Obviously, things were not right between my father and me, but I loved my father. Although he didn't love me, I still loved him. You see, I had no one. I had been dropped off at so many different places so many times before, that to have the chance to be with the person who was my father made me want a relationship with him more than anything. In my mind, with him, there would be no more getting moved around to yet another family.

But I was wrong.

Child protective services took me from my mother right after I was born in 1972, and I was immediately placed in foster care. In 1981, I was finally adopted by my mother's sister and her husband. (Again, this is the father I call "Dad.") From 1981 until 1983, I lived with my aunt and uncle (or Dad). Then for two years, I either lived with my biological father or I survived on my own until 1985. Then, in 1985, while I was living with my grandmother, my father randomly picked me up to go live with him and his wife in Chicago until 1988. For whatever reason, my father never adopted me.

But it wasn't just my fathers with whom things were not right; it was *everyone* who showed me anything but love. I was the family member no one wanted to be around, and I don't know why. I was the house slave, the perfectly placed punching bag, the stress reliever in more ways than one.

Of course, I wasn't perfect. Who is? I was a teenager, trying to get through the growing pains of life while not having my mother. And knowing that she was killed was hard along with watching my father treat his wife's kids better than he treated me. I was the Cinderella of the family.

The other kids—my stepmother's son who was three years my senior and her daughter who was one year my junior—got the best while I got what was left over. If it was old, badly damaged, or just dirty, that's what I got, and at other times, I got nothing at all. I was made to clean everything and eat last—that's *if* any provisions remained for my consumption. I was not allowed to eat at the dinner table with the rest of the family. Instead, I had a small table in a corner, and that's where I sat alone and ate my meals—if you could call them meals. I couldn't eat until everyone else was done, and my plates consisted of bones and the picked-through scraps that were the remnants of the meal they'd had—that's if oatmeal wasn't made for me.

This time in my life was the scariest part of my life.

It was fucked up.

I spent most of my time quietly in a corner or in my bedroom because if I didn't do as I was told, I was beaten. If I didn't clean, eat all my food, or pronounce a word correctly when reading, I was beaten. I was beaten for almost everything. And when I wasn't quietly staying to myself, my father would beat me for making the noise that simply comes from being a child. Quite honestly, he didn't need a specific reason to beat me; he would beat me just because he could.

But in spite of all that my father had done to me, I was still willing to love him because he was blood. He was kin. We were biologically connected. It was so conflicting, though. I understood that a man is supposed to stand up for his family, so I couldn't simultaneously understand why he didn't nurture, protect, and stand up for me. I am his family, too! I'm his biological son, not the other children, his stepchildren! But I was still willing to love him.

During the summertime, my stepbrother and stepsister would play basketball with friends in the yard, but I was not allowed to join them. Instead of getting to go outside and enjoy the months-long break from school, I was made to stay indoors and read the Bible for hours a day every day. Because I was deemed by my stepmother to be a prostitute's child and a demon, she believed I had spirits in me that required me to always keep the Bible in my hand. And if I wasn't reading the Bible, then I had to clean and do chores I guess because, in following with this line of thinking that I was supposedly a demon, idle hands are the devil's workshop, and I could not be allowed downtime for any reason.

One day, while my stepmother's son and daughter were outside playing, per usual, I babysat the youngest child, a three-month-old whom they had adopted, while I read the Bible aloud to my stepmother. This day was no different than any other day until, out of the blue, she asked me if I had a picture of my mother.

Confused, wondering why she would ask me this but also not wanting to start any kind of conflict, I feigned innocence and ignorance and said, "I don't have a picture of you, ma'am."

"You don't have a picture of your real mother, the prostitute?"

Hearing that word, that vile characterization of my mother, I looked at her scared and full of fear, not knowing if she was going to do something horrible to me or have my father beat me. So, shaking in my skin, I acquiesced and said, "Yes."

"Go get it. I want to see what trash your father had before me."

Scared and unsure of what she planned to do to me, I obeyed and went to retrieve the only picture I had of my mother. It was her driver's license photo. When I returned with it, my stepmother took it out of my hand, looked at it, and thus began the onslaught of verbal attacks. I heard the most despicable words describing my mother as the lowest of the low.

"She was a prostitute!"

"You're your uncle's son!"

Her tirade accused my mother of using drugs and claiming that, with all the men who were in her life, I was just in the way. Her assault wouldn't let up. She further twisted the knife in my back, telling me if it hadn't been for the government stepping in to remove me from that home, that my mother would have killed me because she didn't want me.

Wow.

I start to feel the cracks forming on the inside.

My whole little world imploded. I thought to myself *Why are you doing this?* as she plowed ahead with her verbal rage, telling me she didn't understand why I held on to the picture because she didn't think that my mother was all that pretty, that no one knew who was my real father (which was 100% not true), and if it wasn't for them—she and my father—then there was no telling where I would be.

As she got up from the dining room table, taking the picture with her, I did the only thing that a child hurting would do. I found the strength, despite being emotionally knocked down, and I tried to get the picture back for it was the only thing that I had of my mother.

"Why are you taking that from me?!" I asked as I began to cry.

I watched this woman take possession of the only thing I still had that my mother had given me. I watched her as she walked into the kitchen, approached the stove, turned on a burner, and looked as if she would set fire to my most precious memento.

In that moment, the day she gave me the picture flashed before my eyes—the colors, the smells, the other children playing around me. I remember how my mother placed that picture in my tiny hands and said "This is me, baby. Now I'm with you everywhere you go."

But now this woman had taken it from me.

I was so hurt.

I lunged and grabbed at her hand, trying again to get it back, but she would snatch her hand out of my reach, refusing to give it to me. As she turned away from the stove, I thought I had some luck, that there was a chance that she wouldn't destroy the photo, but instead of allowing the flames to consume it, she took scissors to it and cut the photo in what felt like a million little pieces to ensure that I didn't get it back or that I couldn't try to tape it together.

I couldn't do anything but run to my bedroom where I sat on my bed and cried and cried until I cried myself to sleep. While tormented, that was the most peace I could have asked for because hours later, I was awakened by the cursing and screaming of my name from the bedroom doorway where my stepbrother stood, telling me to "get the fuck up and come eat." Unsure if I would actually get food this time while also hoping that if I did, that I wouldn't get cold oatmeal flooded by milk again, I went to wash my face and hands.

As I entered the dining room, I saw that we had company; people from my dad's job were over—two couples—so I dug deep, remembered my manners, and held out my hand to greet them. Just as I did so, my father blurted out, "That's my adopted son."

I quickly turned and looked at him with my hand still in mid-air as he continued with "His mother was killed doing drugs."

What the hell?!!!!!
That's not true!
That's not how she died!
What is he saying?
And why is he saying this?!

The man took my outstretched limp hand to shake it, then not bothering to greet the rest of the visitors because my stepmother immediately told me to go sit down, stunned and numb, I went to my space to be by myself on the floor in the corner.

It was halfway through dinner when my stepmother said to my father, in a very caring voice, "Are you going to tell him?"

I thought *Oh shit. Here it comes—something else to hurt me just for the sake of hurting me.*

But for once, for a fleeting moment, I also thought that because we had company, maybe just maybe I would be safe. That was a dream because do you know the man I look like and the one I act like—this very man that I called my father asked me to stand up from off the floor where I was sitting, opened his mouth at the dinner table in front of everyone, and said that I was not his son?! He went on to say he'd promised my mother on her death bed that he would care for me.

BANG!!!!

It was as if I'd been shot in the chest at close range.

As a child, what was I to think?

Who are you, and why am I here?

Who and where is my real family?

Am I your son, or am I not your son?

What is the truth behind how I came to live here?

As if the events of the day before dinner hadn't been enough, now this! At that very moment for the first time in my life, I wished I was dead.

How does a child come back from that? How was I to even find the want or the will to live after that? *Why?* I asked over and over. How could a person want to hurt a child that they so-call loved. I just didn't understand. Now the question was *If I'm not your son, then why do you have me here? Why even try to care for me, have me call you dad, and waste your time doing for me? Why put yourself through that if you're going to treat and regard me like this?! Why am I alive?*

It seemed with everything my father said and the way he said it, it was as if he wanted some sort of recognition or kudos for coming to my aid when no one else would. I looked up at him with teary eyes and a shaky voice and said, "Thank you, sir."

He angrily asked, "'Thank you' for what?!"

My reality was bleak. I was a motherless child who was not wanted, who was not loved. All this was combined with being hurt over and over again, humiliated, and feeling I was left with no other options. You see, if my own family didn't give a damn about me, then where was I to go? Who else would want me? Who else would take me in? I had no idea what was the right thing to say, but my young mind found some words.

I meekly said, "Thank you, sir, for taking me in."

"You're welcome. Now sit down and finish your food." He paused then said "Thank you—" letting the end of it hang in the air, waiting for me to finish the additional expression of gratitude.

Again, he said, "'Thank you' what?"

I dropped my head, scared to look at him, but after hearing his tone and understanding what he was waiting for, I said in a low voice "Thank you, sir, for the food." And I sat down, slowly giving up, praying that he just beat me to death—that would have been preferred because, that way, I could be with my mom who loved me.

This is the part no one tells you about. This is the part that doesn't make it onto the evening news, and it's why you see people on the streets as you ask yourself "Why won't they go to a shelter?"

CHAPTER 3

The Meeting

Most days, I walked around, looking like a zombie— another dark moment in my life when I wished to just die. I begged God to just kill me. I really didn't want to be out there, living on the streets, but I didn't have what I needed to get off the fast-turning merry-go-round. Although I never stopped praying, it felt more and more like I was going nowhere, which made me cry every day as I slipped further and further into an even darker place, and no one cared. It was as if I was invisible, and that, in and of itself, is so disturbing.

I was homeless multiple times with the first time being when I was fifteen years old. It was during that time then again as an adult when I had to leave my sons with their mom and live on the streets that I came across some really good people who were also homeless but who were some of the most awesome people I have come to meet. I would stick close to them, learning all I could of the do's and don'ts of street life. These lessons made it easier to find food—one of the greatest priorities of each day—then make it back to my sleeping spot, which was under a bridge.

The seasons changed, fall turned into winter, and it became very cold—so cold until police advised me to go to a shelter. And after weeks of trying to fight the elements, I made the decision to retreat to a homeless shelter, which ended up being both a good and a bad decision. I was out of the cold, and I had food to eat, warm clothes to wear, and most importantly, a bed to sleep in. But I had to fight for whatever I had. You'll soon see precisely what I mean when I recount for you the time I was beaten up for my winter apparel. In that environment, not only did you have to stand up for yourself, but in some instances, you had to defend yourself from some of the workers in the shelter.

Your safety didn't matter. Shelter workers would turn a blind eye and a deaf ear if doing so would ensure they could get off work on time. It often felt like it was safer to be on the streets than to be in a facility for the homeless. In one particular Washington, DC shelter, there were all kinds of rugged and dangerous people. While I wasn't scared, I became extremely cautious after witnessing some of the most horrendous acts of violence that people committed against one another. And at this shelter, you had to always watch your back. Always.

The shelter had a system where they woke us up at five o'clock in the morning, and we had to be out by seven o'clock no matter the weather. Come rain, snow, or a storm, you had to be out of there by 7 a.m. We had no sit-down breakfast—only fruit and a carton of milk that was handed to you on your way out the door. It didn't matter if you didn't feel well; they had given you a place to lay your head for the night and a bite to eat—plain and simple; this wasn't your home, and they weren't running a clinic or a hospital. So, even if you were ill, it didn't matter; they had done their job, and by seven o'clock, you needed to head out the door.

But one snowy day, with weather that was so bad until we were told that it was unsafe to let anyone go outside, we were stuck indoors and subject to falling victim to whatever sick notions folks had running through their minds. Case in point, I saw a group of guys that chose another guy as their target, taking his food and pushing him around until they decided to beat him up. I thought *What the fuck?!* There was no hiding my shock and surprise, and my reaction registered with an older homeless guy who was sitting with me.

"Young buck, don't move. Don't leave this room. They're looking for someone to fuck. Don't let it be you."

I took in everything he said.

"Sit here with me, and they won't mess with you."

So, I sat and didn't move.

In no time, it was clear that he knew the drill—that one guy they had been messing with went to the restroom, and all six guys followed him and raped him. I knew then and there I had to always remain aware.

But one morning, as I was getting up to leave, a group of guys got the drop on me, cornering me in the stairwell, beating me up, striking me over the head with a hard object that knocked me out, then taking my winter coat, shoes, and hat. The only silver lining is I was grateful that I wasn't also raped.

One of the shelter administrators found me lying in the stairwell, and his response to seeing me there was to wake me up and tell me to leave. I explained what had happened, hoping for a modicum of sympathy and understanding. But I was sadly mistaken. He looked at me with deep disgust and spat, "I can't do anything to help you!"

I asked if he could at least give me a coat, a reasonable request, I thought, considering my circumstances, the season, and if nothing else, the fact I was in a place that was dedicated to serving the needy.

"I can't help you, and even if I could, I wouldn't. So, get the fuck up and out of the damn building."

My flabbergast was immeasurable, and the worst part was I couldn't do a thing but comply because if I didn't, the police would be called. And once they arrived, I already knew they would just brush me off, not listen to my plight, and maybe even arrest me. I know this may sound like a leap. *How can he jump to such a conclusion* is what you're thinking, right? *Aren't police sworn to serve and protect?* Yes, they are, but I was also a homeless, dirty, stinky man. And the general school of thought was such a class of citizenry deserves any and all manner of wrong done to them.

Police, homeless shelters, and others can paint with a broad brush, assuming all homeless people must have substance abuse problems because no one in their right mind would want to be in a shelter. There's no way a clean person would allow themselves to end up with this kind of life. If only they knew the whole story…

I had no choice but to let the incident go and follow the rules so, if for no other reason, I would be allowed to return for another day. And I knew if I made any further mention of the incident, there was a very good possibility that I could get badly hurt in the middle of the night. It was in my best interest to just shut up and do whatever they said—besides, the alternative was hard, one that meant trying to stay awake while walking the snow-filled streets, physically exhausted and too tired to keep my eyes open.

It was more or less a prison, and in a prison atmosphere, you must never get caught sleeping. I mean it! In that kind of system, one thing is certain, and that is the fact that they will come in the middle of the night when you least expect them—the sheltered turned predators—and I didn't want to die in a homeless shelter.

On top of the safety issues, it was one of the nastiest shelters that I have ever seen in my life. It was like a setting in a *Saw* movie. The cringe-worthy, dirt-laced bathrooms were living and thriving petri dishes. I never used the bathroom while there. I couldn't. The showers had black mold all over everything, and I swear the mold appeared to move. If you touched a surface, you wanted to peel off your own skin to avoid possibly turning into a mutated monster of some sort. The floor of the shower was covered with mounds of wet newspaper and used condoms, and it looked as if someone with a cold had spit green mucus everywhere—showering was out of the question.

This is the part no one tells you about. This is the part that doesn't make it onto the evening news, and it's why you see people on the streets as you ask yourself "Why won't they go to a shelter?" The option to just keep on their clothes and be dirty is preferable to subjecting themselves to what awaits behind shelter doors.

I wanted to be with my children; I wanted to get back to my sons. I needed to find a way out of this mess. But for right now, I needed a coat. So, I walked 2.6 miles in the sneakers that the shelter finally gave me. As I made my way through the snow in twenty-degree temperatures, I intermittently stepped into the entryways of stores and various buildings to get warm. On one of these stops, at a store on First and Florida Avenue NW, a short man approached me asked what I was doing out without a coat.

"I'm on my way to Bread for the City on Seventh Street Northwest to get a coat. I got jumped, and some guys took my coat."

"I see you got it good in the eye," he replied.

My right eye was starting to swell. My left eye was already swollen shut and bleeding in the corner.

"Man, I'll tell you what," he began. "You will die before you get there. It's too cold."

"I have to at least try."

His response was "Well, you can't beat a man for trying."

It was at this moment that he turned to squarely face me and said, "I'm going that way. You can have my coat."

What?!

Why!?

Oh, God. He wants something from me!

I had learned that both in the shelters and in the streets, the same rules apply: Don't take nothing. Don't give nothing.

I got a closer look at him, and that's when I realized he was homeless just like I was only he was a whole lot cleaner. This homeless man gave me one of his coats that he had on, asked me if I wanted some coffee, and handed over a cup before I could say "yes" or before I could object, then he paid for it.

Since he was headed in the same direction, he walked with me, asking a ton of questions like why I was homeless and where was my family. I answered all his questions, and before parting to go our separate ways, he told me his name was Calvin. He'd lost everything after his wife died, and he now lived under the Anacostia Bridge. He told me if I ever needed anything to come check him out. I laughed and said "okay," then asked what time it was. He pulled out a beautiful gold pocket watch and said it was 10:45 a.m. (I eventually learned that this was quite common for a homeless person to have something that reminds them of where they came from or of what they once had.)

Before taking leave of me, he made sure to tell me that he wanted his coat back—a nice heavy twill overcoat—and that

I should bring it back once I replaced the one that had been stolen from me. His specific directions were to bring the coat to the Good Hope Road side of the Anacostia Park under the bridge at the mouth of the park. I gave him my word that I would do so. He then gave me a two-handed handshake, looked me in my eyes, and said that he was jumping off the ride and that I would be safe. He even made me promise him that I would be safe and not get into any trouble. Although I was well into my thirties, I looked far younger than my actual age, so I partially understood his concern; but I didn't fully understand why he was doing all that for and expressing such kindness toward someone who was a stranger to him. I didn't understand why he cared so much. Nonetheless, I gave him my word that I would go straight to the clothing bank and nowhere else. He walked off, going down Seventh Street toward China Town while I kept walking up Seventh Street toward O Street.

Ten minutes later, I entered through the doors of the clothing bank and got a coat. It was so cold, and I didn't have the money to take a cab to make the journey back to see Calvin and instead decided to stay at the Community for Creative Non-Violence (CCNV) homeless shelter, which was not too far away. The snow was coming down hard, my sneakers were wet, and I still didn't have any boots yet, so the option to leave again to return Calvin's coat and risk getting frostbitten feet was out of the question. However, it bothered me so badly that I couldn't keep my word to Calvin due to the snow, but I just couldn't risk it.

Four days passed, and due to the extreme weather advisory, we were still snowed in at CCNV. While sitting on my bunk bed in the basement, we received a visit from several well-dressed men who came in with bags and hot trays of food. They set up tables in the far corner of the left side of the room, and the security officers told us to line up so we could get a hot meal. As we lined up for food, they handed out bags that each contained socks, a winter hat, gloves, underwear, a toothbrush, and a bar of soap. I was so hungry to the point I went back three times! I hadn't eaten in days, and I didn't know when I would eat again so I took a plastic bag, dumped extra food in it, and stuck it in my coat pocket.

One of the guys noticed my outfit, that I was wearing shorts and sneakers, and he asked me if I had any other clothes. When my reply was "no," he looked at me and said, "Come with me. I know you don't trust nor know me. I just want to help. This is why we are here. We want to help you guys."

So, I followed him as he took me to his truck that was parked outside. He asked what size pants I wore and upon telling him, he gave me two pairs of jeans that he had planned to take to the cleaners. He also took off his boots, gave them to me, and put on the sneakers I had on. I was in awe! They were so dirty and stinky, causing me to ask if he was sure that he wanted to do that.

"You're my brother," he said.

My heart burst open, and I began to cry. The man reached out, opened his arms wide, and hugged me.

He said, "We've all gotten lost one or two times in life before we get it right, but you must get up now and take your life back."

He went on to tell me that I can do it, and it will happen with one step at a time. We soon went back inside, and it was after he had departed that I realized I didn't know his name. I asked the security officer if he knew any of their names, but he didn't know either; he only knew that they were masons. I would soon have to leave the shelter so I would not see these men again; but I had hoped I would so I could ask what a mason was.

I knew I had to return to a shelter that was on the other side of town because, at the time, CCNV was limited in capacity. We were in the basement, and it was packed; so, I was among those men who were taken to other shelters that could accommodate us. Where I landed was at a shelter on the other side of DC because while there were shelters that were closer to CCNV, none of them had the space to take me in.

On the day when I decided to leave, it was windy and still bitterly cold, but it was not raining or snowing so that made it a fairly nice day with conditions good enough for me to try to return Calvin's coat. It had now been eight days since our meeting, and I was so happy to be able to finally keep my word and say "thank you" to Calvin. As I arrived at the location he'd described, I saw a make-shift house under the bridge.

I called out for him. "Hey, Calvin!"

No answer.

I called out again.

Still no response.

I waited for hours; nobody came, so I left and returned the next day. For three straight days, I did that—showing up, calling out his name, and getting met with silence.

On the fourth day, before I could call his name, I walked up to find other homeless guys taking Calvin's stuff.

I cried out, "What are you doing?!"

One tall guy replied, "Hey, it's okay. The police said we have to take it down."

"Why?"

"Because Calvin died."

Wait.

What?

I was in a state of shock. The guy continued, obviously having already dealt with his grief, and asked me if I was a mason.

"No, I'm not."

That's when he said Calvin was a mason and that he knew a lot of people.

"The dude got more friends than me!" he said.

They all laughed as I remained blown out of the water, wondering how they were able to laugh right now. I didn't know what to do after that, so I gave the guy Calvin's coat. He commenced with checking the pockets, pulling two one-hundred dollars bills out of the inside pocket. He asked if the money was mine. I said "no," that it was Calvin's.

He then asked, "Did you know it was in there all this time?"

"I had no idea it was in there."

"Why didn't you check the pockets?"

I explained to him how Calvin loaned me the coat to wear until I got one of my own, that my stance was since the coat was not mine, I had no right to search through its pockets.

The guy stood up straight and said, "Wow. My father must have liked you!"

He handed me the $200, turned, and walked away.

I didn't know what to do. All I knew was Calvin, a total stranger, had given me his coat, bought me some coffee, and cared enough about me to promise him that I would stay out of trouble and be safe. And now, in his death, he had given me money to get by. I was overwhelmed and so deeply touched by him for trusting me that I hurried behind a building on Good Hope Road and cried.

I didn't have an address. I didn't have clean clothes to wear. I didn't have a lot of the basics, and I pondered all of this over and over in my head to the point that it made me feel a strong sense of hope for myself.

CHAPTER 4

A Turning Point

It was eleven o'clock on a cool November morning. I made my way to The Big Chair located at the corner of Martin Luther King, Jr. Avenue and V Street Southeast in Anacostia near the Department of Social Services office building so I could use their Wi-Fi. I logged on and, using my iPod and my Google Voice number, called my sister. She was happy to hear from me, but she didn't offer any help. At the same time, I didn't immediately ask for any help either because I didn't want to hear any excuses as to why she couldn't lend me a hand. I thought to myself that by now, I should be used to things being that way since that's what my family does.

That conversation centered around what she was dealing with at the time, which I understood was a big deal, but I expected her to understand that I'm her brother, that I needed her help at that moment. That call didn't last long.

At one point on the call, I finally told her I needed help. And it wasn't as if she didn't already know I needed help. She'd known for some time because I would call and talk to her at least once a week. But my family is like that—they call me only when they need something, and I oblige, getting things done, no questions asked. But if I need anything, my request falls on deaf ears. It's as if I'm asking them to throw a pool party for cats. It's impossible. So, yes, I eventually asked for help on the call, but she acted as if I had said nothing and kept talking about what was going on with her. After a while, you ask once, and if you get nowhere with the ask, you leave it alone.

I soon disconnected, then called my first ex-wife, Adrianna, to speak to her and my eleven- and nine-year-old sons, Royce and Xavier. Though we didn't get along as a married couple, we still had enough respect and care for each other where we could give sound advice and encouragement or so I thought at the time. (I would later find out that that part about us having mutual respect for each other wasn't entirely reciprocated by my ex. The details behind me realizing this do not matter. The bottom line is you live and you learn.)

Adrianna asked how I was doing, and I felt the care in her words. She soon asked if I would come over for Thanksgiving, and I said I would. I explained how I had been living outside, that I was dirty and stinky and that I might even have lice. She wasn't one bit deterred, saying she didn't care about that because no matter what, I was still her friend, and nothing would change that. She comforted me as soon as I started crying. I finally found the composure to tell her again that I would come for Thanksgiving, adding that I would not stay long, and she was okay with that.

"Come by ten o'clock," she said. "That way, you can take a bath and spend time with the boys. You know they need you, right?"

I told her I realized that. We talked a few more minutes, and she prayed for me and told me she loved me. Addressing me by my nickname (pronounced Sa sha), her last words to me were "Sashjaa, be safe, please!" I told her I would do what I could, and there erupted an uncomfortable silence, which I broke by saying "Peace!"

I hung up as she cried. I knew her tears were not brought on because she thought I was a bad person; at the time, that's what I thought her crying was communicating—that she thought I was corrupt and of ill-repute. However, I've come to realize her tears were brought on because I didn't openly acknowledge the fact that she was trying to help me with her words, that she was trying to push me to be better. At the time, I didn't express any appreciation for her showing empathy and care for me. I now know better, but at the time, I didn't understand her feelings. I didn't appreciate and fully understand on a deeper level both spoken and unspoken words.

As I put my iPod back into my pocket, the reality of my situation dawned on me; suddenly, it all rushed back in, hitting me hard, returning me to battle mode. I couldn't let anything, including a heartfelt call with the mother of my sons ahead of the holiday season, take me off my game of surviving.

The next morning, I rolled up my bed, packed up my cart, and started my day by walking down to McDonald's to get coffee and a sandwich. I had an optimistic feeling that something good was going to happen for me, and it caused me to feel extremely positive even as it started to rain. It was as if the sky was dumping buckets and buckets of water as the rain came down hard and nonstop. I was so wet and cold that it prompted my mind to shift into Superman mode, walking as if I wasn't bothered by the cold or wet weather. I stayed focused so I could fill out applications in search of work, then get back to the old building where I had stayed the night before. Once there, I got out of the cold, dried my clothes, then went to the Shrimp Boat store to ask if I could take out the trash, clean the outside, and sweep the front in exchange for food.

As I swept, I saw what appeared to be money in a pile of trash. Without closely looking at it, not wanting to call attention to my good fortune—that's simply something you don't do when you are among the homeless, not if you want to keep and benefit from your good fortune!—I quickly picked up the paper and shoved it into my pocket. Once I finished my work, the lady behind the counter gave me a bag of food and some money. I exited and went behind the dumpster to examine what she'd given me, and that's when I remembered what I'd stuffed in my pocket while sweeping. It was a hundred-dollar bill!

I made a beeline to the corner store across the street and bought all the food I needed—beans, chips, a honey bun, a Pepsi, and a bottle of water. (I was so grateful to be able to pay for the food with money as opposed to having to work for food.) I also purchased a pair of gloves, a bag of socks and a hat, saving the rest of my money, hoping to make it last as long as possible.

As I left the corner store and headed in the direction where I'd stashed my shopping cart, a man wearing a jacket with a mason symbol on it grabbed my hand and said, "Brother, the community needs you. Please do all that you have to do to come back!" That shook me to my core. He went on about his way, entering the store, but I continued to feel his words as if he was still in my midst as I pushed my cart down the street.

That day ended up being a blessing, and I felt God smiling on me. I found some money to get food and had the perfect place to lay my head complete with no rats, no college students looking to kick around a homeless man, and no police telling me to move on—this could only be God protecting and loving me.

This got me to thinking. I contemplated how I would get back on my feet and how I was going to get a job. I didn't have an address. I didn't have clean clothes to wear. I didn't have a lot of the basics, and I pondered all of this over and over in my head to the point that it made me feel a strong sense of hope for myself.

I made it back to the abandoned building, removed my wet clothes, and hung them up. I took my other clothes and washed them in the tub of an apartment bathroom. I shaved, took a birdbath, and I felt was on my way to getting back. The light at the end of the tunnel was in sight!

In a snap, my whole body went from heavily exhausted to extreme battle mode. But I was not going out without a fight. Not this time!

CHAPTER 5

The New Beginning

The next morning, I awoke to what could have led to some real trouble. Contractors were coming in to work on the abandoned building that I was using as my makeshift home. Their arrival made my next steps very clear: It was time to move on. I quickly dressed, packed up my things, and left out the back. No one saw me, and I was thankful for that because I really didn't want any problems. I didn't need them harassing me or, worse yet, calling the police on me. That's the usual response people have to the homeless when they are found in places they shouldn't be—call the police.

The day was bright, cold, and sunny, and my hopes for a new beginning were so strong that I could have healed the sick if I had touched them. I walked downtown to the Martin Luther King, Jr. Memorial Library to fill out and submit online applications all day. I created for myself something of an office and stayed close by to have access to the Wi-Fi so I could make and receive calls with my iPod and Google Voice number.

I went on interview after interview, and everywhere I went, they either laughed at me or made fun of the way I looked or smelled. Those experiences really got to me and affected my self-esteem. I tried to keep the hopes of a better life as my motivator, but soon, that would go, too, leaving me with a broken spirit, a busted heart, and a bitter attitude. Feeling depleted and defeated after a day of putting in the work with trying to find employment, at the first chance I got, I went into a bathroom, changed my clothes, and went looking for a place to sleep.

As day turned into night, the temperature dropped, and it became frigid. It was so cold—colder than usual. I don't know if it was because I was angry with the world or if it was the weather; nonetheless, what I can say is that it was unbearable. The silver lining that I told myself was "One more night, then I will go see my sons."

As I began to gather paper, dried leaves, and branches to start a fire in a trashcan behind an abandoned house, I made a weatherproof shelter on the stairs leading to the basement door. I was out there all night, neglecting the makeshift house I'd made for reasons I don't recall. But one thing that I do remember that gave me the conviction to bear the night was that I would soon be on my way to see my sons.

I had so much on my mind until I couldn't sleep. I didn't want to be homeless anymore. I needed and wanted a hug from a woman. I needed to lay my head on her breast and hear her say "It's okay. You're safe." I was trying to map my way and find a job. I was thinking of how I was going to dress when I made money, how and where I would live, and how I was going to get my sons. I missed their little arms around my neck, hugging me. Those little voices were life for me. I had too much on my mind to be bothered with sleeping or taking advantage of the shelter I'd crafted for myself. I had much greater work to do.

The next day, I walked at times and jogged at times all the way from northeast Washington, DC to Morningside, Maryland, pushing a shopping cart that contained the remains of my whole life. It was nineteen miles from Montello Avenue to Morningside, and it took me *hours* to make that journey. I started at 5:30 a.m. and finally got there six hours later at 11:30 a.m. I hid my cart in the woods behind a church before proceeding up the street to my sons' mom's house.

When I arrived, I was so tired but not too tired to see my sons! I knocked on the door, and my sons ran to me, hugging me, and took me upstairs to the bath they had drawn for me. Adrianna had purchased some clothes for me to wear, which made Thanksgiving that year much more emotional. I got dressed and came downstairs, and everybody was ready to go.

"Where are we going?" I asked.

My son said, "We're going to Uncle J.P.'s house for Thanksgiving, Dad."

I was surprised and was not entirely ready for this. I had my mind set on spending the day with my sons at their mom's home and didn't want to go to J.P.'s, but Adrianna said it would be okay.

"Come on. Everyone misses you," she insisted.

Slightly convinced, I grabbed my coat and walked out to the car. The ride up to my brother's place was filled with my sons asking me questions about where I'd been and when I would be back to spend time with them. I told them I really didn't know.

"Well, you're here now, Dad," Xavier said.

"Can we go to the basketball court tomorrow?" Royce asked.

"Yeah. Sure. I'm game!" I said.

After several minutes of constant chatter and catching up, a sudden silence fell over us. The abrupt shift from talking nonstop to all of us simultaneously not saying a word caused us to all erupt into laughter as we pulled up to my brother's house.

I got out of the car, and I immediately heard shouts of "Uncle Mark! Uncle Mark!" coming from the front door as all my nephews and nieces came bounding out of the house as if the place was on fire. (This is the family of the aunt and uncle who adopted me.)

They jumped all over me, asking questions like "Where have you been?" and "Can we go with you?" As they dragged me into the house, it almost felt like I was a piece of bread being carried by hundreds of ants. When I walked through the door, the first person I greeted was Renée, my sister-in-law.

"I am so glad to see you," she said with a big hug, and I began to feel a sense of peace within me.

"What's up, dawg!" I heard from behind me.

It was my brother, J.P.

We hugged, and he said "Hey, man. I'm glad you came. Come help me on the grill."

I was like "Okay!"

When I arrived outside, I saw my father dropping a turkey into a huge pot of hot oil.

"Hey, boy. Come here and give your old man a kiss!"

Those were always his words to me. I hugged him, and we started talking about the food. No one mentioned the fact that I was homeless. No one mentioned the fact that they had not seen me in years. No one offered to help me with a place to stay or to sleep even after I said that I was living on the street, which made me a bit sad at the time. I guess the only way I was able to be at peace with this was because

I told myself that was God continuing to keep His hand on me. There was so much about love and how to put in the work to make myself better that I had not learned yet. My family offering me a temporary fix was not what God needed for me in that moment. I had so much work to do, and He knew it, which is why He did not allow family to make any offer to help me although I obviously needed it.

All in all, we had a great time, and at the end of the day, my boys and I were on our way back to Adrianna's house. She made up the couch for me where I was to sleep for the night, and before going upstairs, she turned and said, "Please sleep well, okay?" I told her I would. Then my sons hugged me, prayed with me, and went to bed. But I couldn't allow myself to become fully immersed in the comforts of someone else's home, albeit temporarily, and I commenced to taking all the linens off the couch to make myself a pallet where I slept on the floor since that was what I was used to—the ground—the cold, hard floor.

When I awoke the next morning, to my surprise, both of my sons were on the floor, too, sleeping with one on each side of me. Without missing a beat, they announced "Dad's up! Let's play Xbox, Dad."

As we played, I caught myself looking at them more than a time or two, marveling over how I was so proud of how smart they had become, and man, they were so big and tall! We played video games until their mother came down to cook breakfast, and I was so glad for the interruption because they were seriously kicking my butt in Modern Warfare!

That day, I helped clean the house, I gave instructions to my sons about their shared bedroom, and we talked about not putting things any and everywhere. I told them their things have a place and to put them there. Being homeless gave me a heightened sense of awareness around respect for personal property. The preciousness of a place to call home and all its conveniences and trappings are often taken for granted until they're taken away.

Then Xavier said to me, "Dad, we know you are about to go, and we know you are homeless."

He turned and looked me right in my face and said, "Dad, we need you. Please get it together. Please!"

At that moment, everything stopped, and I was standing in the middle of a spinning room. My heart fell out of my chest. I was crushed by his words. As he stood there, looking me in my face, expressing his love and concern for me, my only response was "Okay. I promise." My words seemed insufficient for the occasion, but they seemed to be exactly what Xavier needed because he then threw his little arms around me, giving me the tightest embrace.

Wow! My son needs me!

As the day went on, I tried to squeeze as much as I could into each little minute, hoping it would maximize my time with my boys. And as fast as I could take a deep breath, it was time to go. I put back on the clothes I'd arrived wearing, hugged everyone, and left. I had to hurry because it was getting late, and it would be hard trying to find a place to sleep in the dark. I really didn't want to go, but I had made the decision before arriving at Adrianna's that I would not overstay my welcome and run the risk of getting too comfortable, that I would visit only for Thanksgiving and the day after, then I would go to a shelter.

And that was the worst thing I could have ever done— choosing to go to a shelter.

Before going into the building to get a bed for the night, I hid my cart behind an old warehouse, but apparently, I didn't hide it well enough. Or someone had been watching my movements because when I returned to retrieve it, all my stuff was gone.

I was disgruntled and unhappy with my decision.

Everything was gone *again*!

I lost everything when I ended up getting put out of the apartment when I was with my ex-wife, Kim. Then I lost everything again when she took the twins. Then again when I couldn't get a job. And again every time my family would act as if they didn't see me ... I can't count how many times I'd lost everything. But this loss was slightly different. It was the first time my cart had been deliberately stolen from me. It was a loss but a different kind of loss that had a different kind of sting.

And on top of that, it snowed. I was in this homeless shelter where the men just kept fighting, cursing, and arguing, and the smell of the feces someone had smeared on the walls was unbelievably unbearable. The first chance I got to leave, I took it and made my way to another shelter, walking ten miles in the cold from Alice Place on one side of DC to Martin Luther King, Jr. Avenue on the other side.

It started to snow again, but thank God I was able to check-in; and by God's grace, I got the last bed. This was a true blessing. After checking in, I went to find my bunk. The lights were off in the rooms, which made the hallway lights super bright. I was kind of glad because my eyes were tired, and I was so sleepy that I almost passed up my room number.

But the exhaustion slightly subsided when I saw my room was right across from the bathroom, and that's *not* a good thing. In some shelters, it was quite common for you to get snatched into the bathroom in the middle of the night where you were robbed, beaten, or raped. Having a bed close to the bathroom made these snatches more convenient and, therefore, increased the probability of you being met with such fate. Against my better judgment but since I was right there, I decided to dip in to use it, which turned out to be a colossal mistake.

Three guys cornered me in the bathroom.

In a snap, my whole body went from heavily exhausted to extreme battle mode. But I was not going out without a fight. Not this time! The head of this little ragtag bunch of thugs wanted to take my boots. But as I placed my back up against the wall, I told them they were not going to take anything from me. I got into a ready stance because, this time, I was prepared to fight for what was mine. In the melee, I broke one guy's nose, and the other guy ran off.

The one remaining aggressor, the ringleader, was left to suffer my wrath. I grabbed him and took out all my years of anger on him; it was by the grace of God that I didn't kill him that night. I couldn't stop myself. The more I hit him, the more I could feel the emotions coming out. With one blow, I felt shame. With a second one, hurt. Then another one landed with the feeling of abandonment. And another had the strike of extreme loneliness. Each day, I died a little, and I was becoming something other than the person I had previously known.

"God, help me, please!!!" I yelled out.

Right at that moment, security and police came into the bathroom and found me beating this guy while the other guy was crying about his nose and swollen face. I was detained while the police and security officers went in search of the guy that had run, finding him hiding in one of the other rooms. The three guys were banned because they had a reputation of robbing other homeless guys in the shelter, but I was given a second chance, being that it was my first fight at that facility. The night manager told me to go to my bunk and to not make a sound or I would get thrown out, too.

I did as I was told, returned to my bunk, climbed up into it, and sat there. As everyone slept, I started to cry—hard and uncontrollably. I tried to stifle my sobs because, in the shelter, it's just like being incarcerated. In either environment, if anyone gets the impression that you're in any way weak, they will come after you.

But I just I couldn't stop. I put my face in my coat, and it was like a dam broke on the inside of me. The tears poured out—they flooded out of my eyes like a running faucet. I felt so lost, so broken, so thrown away. I didn't know what to do but pray.

And so I prayed. I prayed so hard until I became dizzy and light-headed. I just talked to Father God as if He was sitting right here on the bunk with me. I asked God what I had done wrong and what I could do to fix this mess. *Where can I go to have peace?* I was tired of fighting; I was tired of being on the streets. I needed my own place. But I corrected myself and said, "I need You. I'm sorry. I need *You* to fix me. Fix all the broken parts of me, please. Just tell me what to do." And, right there, at that moment, I heard a still calm voice say to me "Central Union Mission."

I stopped praying, looked around to see if anyone was there talking to me, but everyone was still asleep. I looked down to the man in the bunk under me, and he was fast asleep, snoring loudly so it wasn't him. But my spirit knew it was God speaking to me. I wiped my face, laid in my bunk, and said, "Okay. I will find it. I will go. Thank you, Father. Amen."

I had to become soft so I could receive His lessons and His plan for my life. I became a big child in His house, getting taught and groomed by Him.

CHAPTER 6

What Lies Ahead

I hated this same routine.

Wake up.

Get up.

Get out.

That was a standard rule—we had to leave the shelter by seven thirty. But I woke up at six thirty the next morning, more than eager to find Central Union Mission. I was up minutes before the lights came on, and just as the lights lit up the room, the security officer immediately told us it was time to go.

I sat on my bunk, mentally recalling what had happened the night before while also praying, and as I finished with my "amen," I heard two guys in the next bunk talking about Central Union Mission. My head turned so fast in their direction until I am lucky that I didn't break my own neck.

I sat there waiting, listening for an address, but no one said anything about the specific location. I was very cautious about asking any questions because I didn't want to start a fight. So, I waited for one of the guys to leave before I walked over to the guy who remained sitting on his bunk, packing.

"Hey, brother," I started. "Where is Central Union Mission?"

He looked at me and said, "Hey, brother. It is over at Fourteenth and R Street Northwest."

He went on to tell me I could get a token from the front desk to catch the bus or take the breakfast shuttle to So Others Might Eat (SOME) then walk the fourteen blocks to Central Union Mission—which is more like twenty-five blocks when you factor in the other streets that run in between the blocks. As I turned to walk away, I thanked him and told him "God bless you."

"Go get yourself together, young blood; the community needs you" was his reply.

I stopped in my tracks and asked, "What did you say?"

"Go get yourself together, young blood; the community needs you," he repeated.

I thanked him again and took his parting words as a sign that I was on the right path since it was a message that I kept hearing over and over again.

Once I arrived outside, everyone was in a line for breakfast and the shuttle; one shuttle was going to Community for Creative Non-Violence (CCNV), one to Martha's Table, and a third to SOME. I skipped breakfast and opted to immediately jump in the SOME line, not wanting to miss my opportunity to get on my way to Central Union Mission. And that's when the foolishness started. Do you know whenever you make the decision to do better or are on the path to become better, the enemy will show up to push you out of place? It's as if the enemy is there in front of you, wanting you to miss your blessings.

The enemy in front of me at that moment was a guy who was checking people's pockets for money as if it was an official job he'd been hired and authorized to perform by an organization called Me, Incorporated. He came up to me, and I promptly told him to keep going and to leave me alone. Undeterred, he said he was going to stab me to death if I didn't let him check my pockets. I dropped my 180-pound duffle bag and told him again—this time in very clear terms—to keep going and leave me alone.

The guy backed up, looked at me, and said, "Watch your back, nigga. Imma get yo ass."

I turned to look him square in the face and asked, "Have you ever seen the face of God?"

"No."

"Do you want to see Him today?"

And, with that, the guy left me alone.

Mind you, I'm not a badass; that's not who I am. But I can scrap with the best of them if it comes to it, and I have no fear. This is a matter of following the rules of the streets, which dictate you can't show weakness, you can't talk too much, don't take or give nothing from anybody, and you never tell anyone you have money or food stamps.

With the troublemaker out of my midst, I resumed my wait in line. The shuttle pulled up, everyone started to board, and before pulling off, the driver used the intercom to instruct everyone to stay seated, that there was to be no hanging out of the windows, and to keep the windows closed. Besides, it was very cold out, and we really needed to do everything we could to stay warm. The ride was long and slow, and when we finally reached SOME at First and O Streets, I was so glad to get off and start my walk to the mission. I was nervous about the whole opportunity, unsure of what to expect, however, I needed to make this move. I needed to get my sons.

But it looked like everything and everyone was trying to keep me from getting to the mission; it was as if all factors were working against me.

The strap on my duffel bag broke.

The police stopped me, asking for ID.

A reckless driver almost hit me as I was crossing the street.

The closer I got to my destination, the more challenges I faced.

But it didn't stop me.

I finally made it!

I walked up to the door of a large warehouse-looking building. I was so excited as I anticipated the new beginning of my life; however, the moment I touched the door handle, the fear of not knowing the process, what would be asked of me, and whether I would have to fight flooded through my mind. I began to second-guess my decision and was just about to turn and walk away when the door was buzzed to let me in.

Shaken, I walked in, and that's when I wanted to leave more than ever. As I took one step after the next, I looked back so many times, thinking and shaking. It had to have been an angel pushing me farther into the building toward the counter because if it had been up to me, I really think I would have turned around and strolled right back out that door.

I walked up to the counter where a guy was seated.

"How can I help you?" he asked.

"I was told to come here for help."

"What kind of help?" he asked.

"I want to get my life together and get off the streets."

I'm pretty sure the front desk attendant saw me shaking as the look on his face said "Are you sure about that?!"

He excused himself to a back room and returned with another guy, a huge man who was about six foot three and who introduced himself as Bill Simmons.

In a deep voice, he asked, "How can I help you?"

I repeated, "I was told I could get help here." And that's when Mr. Simmons started to explain all the benefits the mission had to offer.

"We have two programs here," he began. "One is STP, which is the Spiritual Transformation Program, and the other is homeless outreach. Which one do you want?"

"STP," I replied.

It was easy for me to immediately choose STP without hesitation and without any explanation of what the program entailed. You see, when I heard God's voice the night before, telling me to go to Central Union Mission, I subconsciously decided that anything with the word "spirit" in its name meant that's what I was there for, that that's what God was pointing me toward. And that was the best decision I ever made in my life—not just entering the program but listening to God.

"Okay," he said, then he asked me to sit in the chapel and wait to speak to Pastor Frazier.

I sat and waited until a short, a gray-haired black man asked me to come into an office where he began to tell me about the program.

I had to stay inside the building for 120 consecutive days.

It was mandatory that I attend chapel.

It was a must that I take the Bible classes that were held every day, Monday through Friday.

I would have chores every day.

I had to help the overnight *guests take showers and get dressed.

Plus, I had to do laundry, engage in food prep, and make the beds.

Although it felt like it was going to be a lot, my response was "Okay. What do I need to do next?"

I was all in.

STP was designed for those who wanted to get back on their feet. It wasn't just for the homeless; there many who came there from jail, too. The mission used Bible teachings to heal a person's deepest, darkest hurts—whether you were struggling with drug addiction, alcoholism, or abuse, STP was there to help and heal. And if you were enrolled in STP, you didn't have to leave the building, which is a great advantage given the average shelter typically requires you to leave each morning, then offers beds that evening on a first-come, first-served basis.

Pastor Frazier told me he would need my cell phone and computer, but I had pawned my iPod that I'd used to make calls via Google Voice, and I didn't have any other electronics; so, we were good on that front. I passed a drug test and was shown where I would sleep.

My things were placed in the locker room where all the personal belongings go. After I locked my things away, I was

---

*These guests were homeless men who were not enrolled in the programs at the mission and who could not stay consecutive nights. They were allowed to stay for only one night at a time and had to sleep in a different area from those who were enrolled in the programs. We referred to them as "guests" because although they were homeless, they were still people who deserved respect and some level of dignity.

escorted back to the chapel and was instructed to a wait there until lunchtime.

Eventually, Mr. Simmons came into chapel and asked me if I was ready to eat. Since I didn't eat breakfast, I was very hungry, and my response was an emphatic "Yes!"

"Come on. Let's eat."

I stood up and followed him into a big cafeteria where everyone was already eating. I was told to get in line, get my plate, and sit anywhere. As I walked toward the line, I saw two large tables filled with all manner of desserts—cookies, cakes, pies, and oh my! I became a big kid wanting everything. I just didn't know what to take! Then there was a juice and water machine and a table next to it filled with fruit. I lost perspective for a moment, stunned by the abundance that surrounded me; it was unheard of for an indigent to have this kind of access to food. I had to look at myself to remember I was a dirty, stinky, broken, homeless man in a room filled with food set for, in my mind, nothing less than a king.

Then there were the entrées. Oh my God! I could not believe what I was seeing—plates with leg quarters, vegetables, and rice with gravy. When the lady handed me my plate, I started crying.

"You're in a great place to be healed," she said.

I looked at her and said "thank you" before walking away to sit at a table with a group of other guys where one of them said "You're new. Man, you're safe now, so don't worry. You're good here."

I said "thank you," then thought he must have seen the look on my face that was a mixture of awe, excitement, as well as the strong tug of fear of the unknown being in this new and strange environment, which prompted his message of reassurance. I didn't understand how I had become so soft. I have always been so hard, and tough—fighting, cursing, out-smarting, and navigating the streets to stay ahead of everyone else—so in real talk, I wasn't a punk by any stretch of the imagination! But now I found myself so sensitive, so vulnerable. This was an emotion I didn't understand, and it was super scary for me.

As I look back on this moment and as I write, I see it was God's plan. I had to become soft so I could receive His lessons and His plan for my life. I became a big child in His house, getting taught and groomed by Him.

After lunch, I was escorted back to the chapel to wait for my next assignment. In came Mr. Jonathan Radcliffe, a well dress black man who looked like he took great pride in his appearance and mannerisms and whose name I would later learn was not just Mr. Radcliffe but Chaplain Radcliffe. I would also later learn he was a resident, too, working to get his life together. And this dude would come to be my best friend, mentor, and a father figure. I love this man with all my heart.

With him was an STP student who was there to show me around and take me upstairs to the library. This place was huge and somewhat intimidating, but the student made me feel at ease so much so until I ended up picking out a book, sitting in a corner to read for so long until the next thing I knew, it was time for dinner. The student had left me to myself and returned to take me to the cafeteria. And once again, it was an awesome spread.

"Hey, brother," I said to the man in line in front of me. "Is it always like this?"

"No. They don't have the other table with the fruit tarts," he said.

"What?!! So, it's like this all the time for the most part?!"

"Yes!" he exclaimed.

Damn! I'd hit the jackpot!!

Immediately after dinner was chapel. We entered, sat down, and had church. And I really needed it. I needed to hear and feel God's love for me. I was overjoyed. Feeling the warm hug God gave me was the best that I had felt in a long time. Once service came to an end, I was escorted to my bunk, then to the showers. The student advised that we must all take showers each night with no exception, so I showered, dressed, and went to lie in my bunk, feeling ready for what the next day would bring. I was ready … until the lights went out, and that's when the fear set in.

This was my routine for several days, and it wasn't until they felt I was ready that I was fully enrolled and immersed into STP. And it was a great experience because it was Bible all day, every day. The mission gave me a Bible, and we could not walk around without it. We were instructed to read it and be ready because at any time, anyone could walk up and ask a question that we were obligated to answer. Others may have found this to be daunting, but I thought it was super cool!

Here was the set-up:

5 a.m.:	Wake up, get myself together—brush my teeth, wash my face, and get dressed to go down and wake up the overnight guests.
6 a.m.:	Wake up the guests, then change the linens, sweep and mop the sleeping quarters, clean the bathrooms, sweep and mop the stairs, and send the laundry down to the laundry room.
7 a.m.:	Go to breakfast.
7:30 a.m.:	Attend devotion.
9 a.m.:	Attend the first class of the day, Fruit of the Spirit.

12 p.m.:	Have lunch.
1 p.m.:	Attend the second class of the day, How to Study the Bible, as well as 12 Steps. When it came to 12 Steps, I didn't have a substance abuse problem, so I focused on forgiveness, hurt, abandonment, mental and sexual abuse to help me address what fueled my anger.
4 p.m.:	Engage in independent studies where we spend time individually using what was taught in class that day to engage in further learning and growth.
6 p.m.:	Have dinner.
7 p.m.:	Attend chapel.
9 p.m.:	Help the overnight guests up to the sleeping quarters and get them ready for the showers.

Once every guest was showered, an STP student read scriptures, and another prayed. STP students then went to our quarters at which time we studied, showered, and retired to bed. This was the routine Monday through Friday; there were no classes on the weekend, but housework was doubled—there was a mission in the mission.

*The heaviness
of the world was
lifted, and I could feel
the weight dropping
off. It was so extreme
and overwhelming that
I buckled and fell to
the floor—my legs had
to adjust to no longer
having to hold up so
much weight. It was like
I had to learn to walk
all over again.*

CHAPTER 7

The Encounter

"Why are you always so angry?"

That was the question I was met with on a bright new day at the mission during my fourth week there. I was sitting at the front desk, checking-in guests, when Chaplain Radcliffe approached me with this query.

"I'm not always angry," I told him.

That was when he said, "You are angry now."

"I'm not angry."

But to be honest, I *was* angry.

Then he said, "You have to surrender that to God for you to be healed. You do know that this is part of the program."

"I'm good," I replied.

But he said, "No, you are not." And this is the part that changed my life forever. "Come with me, my brother. Come on, come on."

So, I got up, and he took me into the prayer room that's just off the chapel. It was a room I'd never been in, a room that was the size of a small office with a total of four rows of chairs on both sides. And down front was a wall-sized lighted glass mural of Jesus Christ with His arms and hands stretched wide and angels, birds, and all kinds of beautiful colorful images gathered around His image. Right below it was an altar, and to the left, was a bookshelf with Bibles on it. In front of the altar was a small podium. The room was painted in a light peach color and had brown carpet. Everything else was a cherry wood, and there was a fragrant, pleasant smell that was—in a word—awesome. It was the perfect place to sit and have a conversation with God.

My instruction from Chaplin Radcliffe, as we entered the room, was I needed to surrender to God the Almighty and that I was not to come out of the room until I had done so. Chaplin Radcliffe then turned and walked out, closing the door behind him.

I was definitely angry at this point, sitting in the prayer room with my arms crossed, pouting like a five-year-old child. Yep, there was no doubt about it—I was acting stupid. So, I was sitting there angrily, aimlessly gazing around. I glanced up at the image of Jesus and made a grunting, dismissive sound, then closed my eyes and went to sleep.

Ten minutes passed when Chaplin Radcliffe entered the room again, took one look at me, and said, "You are not ready," then closed the door before I could say anything.

That got to me! It made me stand up and yell out to him through the closed door, "I don't need to be in here!"

He yelled back, "Surrender and give it to God!"

I sat down, boiling inside and angrier than before. I looked up at the mural of Jesus and barked, "So, You want it, huh?! You want it? Well, You got it!" as I threw a chair across the floor. It was a moment I would never forget.

Ever!

"I'm locked in this damn room because of You!" I muttered.

"It was all good. I was minding my own business, and now You want me to surrender?! Didn't I come here like You told me to? And now You want me to surrender? So, You want all my burdens? So, You want them?!"

At this time, I was looking up at the mural of Jesus and said in the most disrespectful manner a man could ever speak to the King of Kings, "Why didn't You help me when I was out there trying to find food to eat?!

Where were You when random guys beat me up in the stairs and took my coat and I had to go out in the freezing snow?!

Why am I alone, by myself?!

Why didn't You stop my wife from cheating on me?!

Why did You let my father beat me up the way he did, breaking my jaw and arm?! He broke my body and my spirit, and You did nothing!

Why was I abused sexually, mentally, and physically?

Why, damn it, why?!

Where the fuck were You!?

Why am I homeless?

Why doesn't my family love me?

What did I do for them to not to want to be around me?

Why doesn't *anybody* want me?!"

I kept on yelling and ranting at the top of my voice. As my yelling got louder, tears burst from my eyes and rolled down my face, and I shook my fist at the mural of Jesus.

"Where the hell were You when I was being molested?!" I continued.

"How the fuck could You let that happen?! Why won't You answer me? ANSWER ME, damn it! *WHY DID YOU LET THAT MAN KILL MY MOTHER!* Why?!!"

And then it happened!

The heaviness of the world was lifted, and I could feel the weight dropping off. It was so extreme and overwhelming that I buckled and fell to the floor—my legs had to adjust to no longer having to hold up so much weight. It was like I had to learn to walk all over again.

Now on my knees, looking up at the mural, I felt like I had just been through a war.

"I'm sorry for cursing at You," I began.

"I'm sorry for not being what You wanted me to be.

I'm sorry for not doing what You asked of me.

Please forgive me.

Forgive me, Father, for fighting all the time.

Forgive me for being abusive with my words and my hands to those around me.

Forgive me for not forgiving myself, God.

I forgive my father for breaking my jaw, breaking my ribs, and beating me up.

I forgive him, and I forgive my family for mistreating me.

I forgive my wife for cheating on me.

I forgive my molesters in the foster home. I forgive my uncle for molesting me.

I forgive the man that murdered my mom.

Oh! God, I forgive them all!"

I went on and on and on for I don't know how long. When it all came to a final climax, I was lying on the floor with snot, spittle, and tears all over my shirt and the floor as I screamed from the top of my lungs, "I LOVE MYSELF, AND I LOVE YOU, GOD!"

It was so breathtaking. I was hoarse, unable to say another word, lying there on the floor, crying. That's all I could do in that moment was cry. And the more I cried, the more I let go.

I was freed. I felt the weight being lifted off my shoulders, and I witnessed a calming peace that radiated through me.

Then Chaplain Radcliffe came in, picked me up from the floor, hugged me, and said, "It's done. It's okay. God loves you." Our embrace lasted for about five minutes before he told me to go to my room where I laid on my bunk and was out for the rest of that day.

Now, up to this moment, I believed in God, but at the same time, I had my doubts in Him and in His ability to show up when I needed Him. I now see that all of that was intentional; it was necessary for me to learn and experience it all so that I may help others. I went through what I went through to be able to tell and show others there's another way out. It was not all just for me, and I see that now. Thank you, Father, for this. I love You.

There was a distinct difference between her and my foster mother because the woman I had come to call my mom—Mrs. Hill—was white, but here I was with a black woman sitting with me, holding my hand, and telling me how much she loved me.

CHAPTER 8

The Transformation

Here's where I really got put to the test: It was when I started attending technical school. After a year of learning and growing, I completed the Spiritual Transformation Program (STP) at Central Union Mission, then I enrolled in the Building Maintenance Service Technician program, also called BMST, a program that was hosted by So Others Might Eat's Center for Employment Training (SOME CET). My first week of training was a bit challenging to say the least. I was at a point where I didn't know what to do, how to get back on my feet, or how to find my voice in life again. However, I wasn't afraid to confront my fears. I used what I had learned in STP as a guide in the coming months.

I was back in the world with a whole new backpack full of tools to use in almost any situation, knowing my triggers and having the Word of God in and accessible to me. And knowing that I was fully equipped to go through whatever challenge, I realized it would be applying these skills what would be the challenge, which led me to learn to use my heart and open it up to see things through a lens of love.

It was through the application of viewing everything from a side of love that it dawned on me that I needed to put in much more work. I thought I was good and free from reliving the same problems of my past, like getting mad, feeling low, being ashamed, and thinking I was unworthy. I didn't run from any of these emotions, though, when they made an appearance; I remained firm, dug deep, and stood my ground. Even when I was wrong, I still stood my ground. While it may not sound like the wisest thing to do, I did it, making it work to my advantage. Here's what I mean:

It was Day 1, Week 1 of my BMST program, and the teacher asked me to read a paragraph aloud during orientation. This request made me so anxious because I have dyslexia, plus I'd had surgery on a small part of my brain from where I'd had cancer. As a result, when I get nervous, I stutter really badly. Dyslexia plus a stutter—what a combination, right?! The stuttering can get so bad until I can get to a point where I can't even see. So, without divulging all of this in front of the class, I told some quick jokes in an attempt to ease the tension, calm my nerves, and buy myself some time. I took a deep breath, and I was okay, but then, in a flash, the fear washed all over me again. This time, the fear asked "Will I be able to read, talk, or see?" In the end, I got through the reading, but it was not easy at all. After the orientation, I walked around with the thought in the back of my mind that the teacher and my classmates were laughing at me behind my back, and it bothered me for the first two weeks. Even though I was wrong by thinking the worst, I stood my ground, using those emotions to drive me to be better than everyone in the class. I studied longer and harder, took copious notes on everything, tried to be the first to engage in hands-on activities, and I was also fast in completing those tasks, performing them perfectly.

It wasn't until I enrolled in SOME CET that I was able to put into practice all the education from Central Union Mission that taught me to have a spiritual outlook on life. I wish they had taught us how to transfer what we were learning to real life scenarios, though; that way, it would have made things so much better and easier for me. I knew how to use the teachings to work on me but not how to use them to navigate the world outside of me. If I'd understood how to transfer what I'd learned to real life scenarios, I believe I could have made higher grades and could have just relaxed in class instead of being extra in everything I did. But because I struggled to seamlessly apply in my tech classes what I'd learned at the mission, I really had to do a lot of work to deal with my low self-esteem.

Because I was funny, that allowed me to make friends. Plus, I usually dressed in business casual attire or in what most people in my circle would call a "Getting Your Grown Man On" style. All in all, I would say that I was cool and likable, but I was hiding behind the humor and the clothes to mask the fact that I was very insecure about my abilities in everything. The people in my circle saw me as the man who got things done, and they loved to help and be around me. So, I allowed that to fuel my decision to put myself in uncomfortable situations where I would be able to learn and conquer my fear of not being liked or of feeling I was being excluded. I don't know the origins of these feelings and these fears. I don't even know exactly when they developed inside of me, but I can tell you exactly *where* in life it all began and why I was so guarded.

When I was born in 1972, child protective services took me from my mother, and I was immediately placed in foster care. It was in 1976, when I was four years old, that the beatings became part of the punishment. In all honesty, the other foster children in the home and I really didn't have to do much of anything to get a beating or to be made to stand in the corner for pretty much all day. And just because you stood in the corner, that didn't save you from further brutality; you still ran the risk of getting a beating depending on how the person standing in front you felt at the moment. So, for me, there was no wishing for one or the other; there was no picking the lesser of two evils—they were equally bad, especially when Mrs. Hill was not around.

Mrs. Hill was the house mother, and she had five sons; four of them lived in the house with us, three were grown men, and the youngest son was a teenager. There was a total of four foster kids in the house, and we lived on the corner. We kids knew that if Mrs. Hill left, we had to go hide or play quietly until she got back. But no matter what we did—any little thing would piss these guys off. We lived in a great big house in the upper northwest part of Washington, DC. The house was so big that we could play in any part of the house, and you would never know we were there, which is all the more reason why when we screamed from the beatings, no one came to see about us.

We would get beatings from all the sons at different times; there were times that Mrs. Hill couldn't even control them, and we would get beaten anyway. Along with the physical abuse came the verbal abuse. The guys would call us "stupid," "ugly," "monkeys," "dogs," and anything that they could think of to hurt our feelings or break our spirit. They also threw things at us. In simple terms, they just were not nice to us at all, and as a child getting that kind of harsh treatment at that age, it was scary. But nothing was as scary as what happened during the nighttime.

Some nights, the guys would hold me down and grind on me or fondle me. I never knew who it was exactly because they would hold the covers over my head when having sex with me. I told Mrs. Hill, but nothing changed.

No.

Wait.

Something *did* change—it got worse. It was so bad that we foster kids stopped sleeping alone and would all get into one bed together. I remember one night how we held on to each other underneath the covers. Sometimes, we slept *under* the bed, but that didn't stop whoever it was.

After some time, it got to the point where we simply got accustomed to the fact that we knew someone would surely come in the night to assault us, and we would just let it happen. We succumbed. No fighting. No resisting. Because what was the point? And as soon as they were done, they would leave.

I thought this was my permanent home and didn't know that I was in a foster home until one day Mrs. Hill took us to a place where other children were playing with toys and having fun—the local foster care visitation center. We got to go out back on the playground, and I loved going to this place at a pace of what seemed like once a month. There was always a lot of people there—some were celebrating birthdays, and others were meeting their family members for the first time, just like me.

I went a couple of times and sat and talked with a lady who told me she was my mother. There was a distinct difference between her and my foster mother because the woman I had come to call my mom—Mrs. Hill—was white, but here I was with a black woman sitting with me, holding my hand, and telling me how much she loved me. I didn't understand what was going on, but I felt strongly drawn to her. I felt a connection, and I wanted to stay with her. I wanted to be next to her all the time, and I needed to touch her every other minute.

"Please take me with you. I don't want to go with the other lady. I want to come with you," I begged.

But this woman, my biological mother, did not immediately oblige. Instead, she promised me, on one visit, that she would come and take me home one day in the near future. I cried, and she held me, wiped my little face, kissed me, then introduced me to my two brothers.

"I have more brothers?" I asked

"You only have two brothers, baby," she said.

I told my mother about the other foster boys in the house, and having bonded with them, I asked if they could come home with me, too. But she told me that, of those boys in the home where I lived, I was the only one that was hers and that I needed to know that I would be coming home soon. It was from that point forward, every time I went to the visitation center to see my mom, I felt, in order to get away from Mrs. Hill and her sons, I had to prove to my mom I was ready to go home with her.

As a child, I would show her all the things I could do; on some level, I was trying to impress her. I wanted to see if she accepted me for what I could do. I was like "Look, Mom. I can run really fast!" or "I can climb really high on the bars." I was trying to let her see that I was worth taking home. "I can run, talk, walk, and I can learn—just teach me what I need to do for you to want to take me with you" is what I would say every time. I would have done *anything* not to have to go back to the foster house, and I wonder if she knew that. I wonder if she could feel my pain, my fears, and how scared I was to leave her side.

A little of me would die every time she had to go back through that damn gray door. I hated that door—no matter what color they painted it, it still represented the hurt and pain I felt from being left. I would scream and cry, and my mom would say "Don't cry, baby. I will be back. I promise."

But she didn't come back.

My mom was murdered the night before I was to permanently go home to live with her.

An evil man took my every hope from me.

So, the lie my father told me about her succumbing to drugs was just that—a lie.

I still remember the anticipation from that one home visit when I went to my mom's apartment and she showed me my room that I would share with my brothers. The gift she gave me was a book called *The Flower Maker*, and she wrote my full name on the inside cover and on one of the last pages. She took me to my grandmother's house where I met my grandmother, aunts, uncles, and cousins. I felt so much love—the kind of love that I long for even now. All the dreams of her making me pancakes, taking me to the playground, going to get ice cream—all the things that she promised me we would do, this man took from me. He took it all away. He killed me, too. I WAS DEAD!

So, every time I remembered things that happened back then, I would break down. I thought of all the abuse, all the mean and nasty things that were ever said to me. Every punch, kick, or joke made at my expense would fuel the anger in me, and it made me want to fight any and everyone. I just didn't care. And on the days I didn't want to fight, I felt low, worthless, abandoned, thrown away. This is where the low self-esteem came from.

But it was the director at CET who saw through all my hurt and pain. She encouraged me to keep going, to get what I needed to live, and to live awesomely. She was there when I needed to cry, she was there when I needed to scream, she talked to me when I couldn't see my sons because their mother was being mean to me. She was my help.

And then I completed the program. And just like any other special event in my life, no one came. And just like so many other times, I was stopped in my tracks with bad news. The twins' mom, Adrianna, called me and said that she couldn't do it anymore, that I needed to get the boys or she was going to take them and drop them off to the courts. Remembering my own experience with the foster care system, I didn't hesitate to say, "Okay. Bring them to me."

I fast-tracked the process to leave the mission. While everyone said it was a bad idea to do so, I didn't let it stop me because I was going to get my sons. I *had* to get my sons. The plan was to move out of the mission and into a friend's home, and the friend said I could bring my sons with me. I called Adrianna, and before I could get barely the words out of my mouth, she was dropping them off along with all their belongings. It didn't matter if their clothes were clean or not, I had them, and I was not going to ever let them go again. My twins—who were five years old at the time—and I were back together, and I was going to do whatever it took to protect and provide for them.

*Did my family know
I was homeless?
Yes!
Did they know my
marriage was rocky,
and I needed help?
Yes!
Did I call out for help
many times?
Yes!
But I just didn't matter.*

CHAPTER 9

Refused and Limited

When my mom was murdered, I was adopted by an aunt—my mother's sister—and my aunt's husband, but I never really felt like family. Watching how my family members were and how they were treated, loved, honored, and celebrated always put me in a very sad place because I wanted that, too. You know—that hug just because; those words of encouragement when you feel bad for dropping the ball, making a mistake, or failing at something that you worked so hard on; the call when it's your birthday, Father's Day, any holiday, or just because—I would love that! But instead, I'm the one who calls, and when I do, it's "I'm busy," "I can't talk right now," or "I can't help you." I seem to have tried all I can just to get attention.

Growing up, I was super funny, animated, nice, caring, attentive. I was always helping, but I couldn't get anyone to show up for me. It's a very hurtful feeling. My biological father would say and do some of the meanest things to me, and I just didn't understand. Neither my biological father nor my adoptive dad was truly there in my life.

All I wanted was love and attention from my biological father like all the other kids in the family were getting. I watched my cousins and their dads, and I would try to insert myself into their activities. I wanted my father to love me the way my friends' dads loved them. I longed for it. I needed it. I would follow my father around and do whatever he was doing; I wanted to be just like him.

My mom was gone, and I relied on a father who wanted nothing to do with me—and he showed it in everything he said and did. If he was sitting on the couch and I came and sat down beside him, he would make me so uncomfortable with emitting sounds and twisting up his face to express his annoyance with me to the point he would eventually get up to move—that's if he didn't curse at me first, making me feel worthless.

I remember a time he, some of his friends, and the friends' kids were in the basement, playing pool. In between taking shots, one of my father's friends would play with his girlfriend's kid, and I wanted to play with them, too. My father was there, too, with his girlfriend, now wife, but he wouldn't play with me. And although the guy told me to stop playing with him, I couldn't understand why I needed to stop. I thought we were having fun; besides, he was playing with the other kids, my father wasn't playing with me, and I wanted to join in on the fun, too!

That's when the night turned bad.

This man, whom I respected, took off his belt and beat me with it. I'm not talking about a couple of whips but an all-out melee on me.

And my father just stood there and said nothing.

I looked at him as I called out for his help, waiting and hoping for someone—*anyone!*—to intervene.

I looked at him.

You're letting this man all-out beat me like a dog in the street, and you and your girlfriend are not going to say or do something?!

So, as this family "friend" was about to bring down his last strike to me, he yelled out, "I SAID LEAVE ME ALONE AND STOP PLAYING WITH ME!!"

Then my father coolly said, "He told you to stop."

What?!!

Regardless of whether I stopped or not, you're my father, and you're supposed to protect me. Why won't you just spend time with me so I won't have to go in search of attention from someone else?! Damn, dude. I'm ten, and I just want to be with you and like you. And you just stood by and let another person straight dog your son!

I was this man's only biological son, but he let this happen to me. I felt so hurt, so left out, and disregarded, but it wouldn't be the last time. There was plenty more to come when we all moved into a big house with his mom—my paternal grandmother—and he and I lived in the basement.

My father would beat me in that basement all the time, and no one would come help. I would tell my grandmother that my dad would punch on me and throw me around, but revealing this to her seemed to bring about no positive change. She would talk to him, of course, but the only change that would happen was he would just punish me by giving me another beating or make me stay in the house and not go outside at all. And do you know that after he left to move away with his wife and her kids, leaving me to live with my grandmother, that he then gave his brother license to beat me?

My uncle would come home in the middle of the night, drunk, and would beat me, and no one would come downstairs to my aid. I told anyone who would listen. I told Rob, my grandmother's boyfriend. (Although he was not married to my grandmother, I still call him Granddad because he helped raised me, and he earned the title.) He stepped to my uncle, and that stopped the mistreatment but only when Granddad was around. When he wasn't around, it was business as usual. I would have never thought that things could get any worse, but they did.

When I was fourteen, my biological father returned to DC and asked me to come live with him in Chicago, and because it was my father, I said "yes." But he also came with gifts and apologized for the way that he had mistreated me, punching me repeatedly in my grandmother's home and beating me up for telling my aunt how badly he had treated me. This man looked me in my eyes and said that he was sorry, and I believed him.

We went to Chicago, and after the first week of fun, laughs, and good times passed, it was hell on earth. Nothing I did was right. I was always cleaning and always in the house, babysitting a child they had adopted and whom they would tell everyone was their child while saying I was the one who was adopted.

This disregard and denial of me, in my mind, was partially what fueled my father's wife's decision to engage in inappropriate behaviors with me. She would fondle me and show me her naked body, making me touch her back. And one day she tied me up and had sex with me, threatening me that if I revealed any of this to anyone, she would tell my father to kill me. I was scared because my father didn't hold back the punches with anything concerning me. So, this went on a few more times where she made me have sex with her, and if I didn't, she would find a way to take it.

While nothing about this was healthy nor was it normal, I was still a human, warm-blooded heterosexual male teenager; and I started liking that way she would make me feel. Everything in me knew that it was wrong. Everything. And because I knew it was wrong from the start, I finally found the courage to tell her that this had to end, that I was going to tell my father. And that's when she said the words that would almost end my life.

"I will tell your father that you raped me, and he will believe me before he will believe you!"

I was stunned.

Flabbergasted.

Deflated.

Defeated.

Broken.

As she untied me from the bed, all I could do was numbly lie there, paralyzed, eventually falling sleep.

The next morning, around eight o'clock, my father burst into my room as I was waking up. Still resolved that I was going to tell him everything, I said, "Dad, I need to talk with you—" But before I could finish my sentence, he punched me in the face, breaking my jaw. I screamed in pain, but he was just getting started. He threw me across the bed and commenced to punching and beating me like I was a grown man and we were at war. With every hit, I could feel bones breaking in my ribs and my arm as he yelled "You raped my wife!"

I was only a teenager. I was little and skinny. And at the time, she was in her forties.

Come on, man. Do you truly believe I overpowered your wife? Really?!

And as if this wasn't bad enough, her son came in, and he started beating me. I couldn't say anything. My mouth was filled with blood, and I was holding my jaw with my hand. After some time, he grew tired and inflicted further pain with his words as he started to yell out my new restrictions.

1. I could no longer eat meals with everyone.
2. I was no longer allowed to eat any food that was bought for the house.
3. I could no longer wear the clothes that he'd bought me.
4. I could no longer stay in my room. I had to sleep on the floor in the basement.
5. I had to leave at six o'clock every morning when he left.
6. I could return only after he arrived home at seven o'clock in the evening.
7. And I could no longer enter and exit the house through the front door; I had to use the back door.

When he was finished, he picked me up and thew me down the stairs onto the basement's concrete floor, and that's when I felt a snap in my leg as he slammed the door shut. It was the dead of winter, the basement was cold as could be, and I had on nothing but a tee shirt and shorts—I was so cold. And I was so hurt by him and what had just happened.

Why do I always get the short end?

It was in that moment that I told to myself that if God were to let me live, I would bulk up and no one—not even my father—would ever hurt me again. I balled up in the corner, and shortly thereafter, I heard the car start up. From the window, I could see the car leaving, going down the driveway, and a few minutes later my father's wife came down to the basement.

"I told you he would believe me. And when I tell the family, no one will listen to you. They already don't like you. Your grandmother didn't want you, and your mother didn't want you. So, you will die all alone like your mother did." Then she retreated up the stairs, laughing at me.

At 5:30 the next morning, my dad yelled down the stairs, calling my name, throwing clothes at me, and telling me I had five minutes to get dressed and out of the house. I was barely able to lift my arms let alone stand up and put on clothes. I rushed as best I could to get dressed because I didn't want to give him any reason to beat me again.

Again, he yelled, this time saying, "It's time to get out of my house!"

I hobbled up the stairs, out the door, and into the freezing Chicago morning cold, walking the streets until eight o'clock when I went to my friend's, Chris's house. I told him what had happened, and he let me stay there for a few days. Chris's brother was the head of one of the gangs in Chicago, and he wanted to hurt my father and stepbrother, but I begged him not to.

Chris's brother's words were "What kind of man does this to his son? You're my family now, and I need to deal with him."

I said, "We are not related."

And he turned to me and asked, "Don't you call my little brother your cousin?"

"Yes."

"Anybody that's family to my brother is *my* family."

And I begged him again, telling him that I would go back to DC, that I would do anything.

"Please don't kill my dad!" He finally gave me his word that he wouldn't.

After a couple days, one evening around eight o'clock or so, I walked to a payphone at a gas station to call my grandmother in DC so I could tell her what had happened. I guess I could have called from Chris's house, but at the time, I didn't know anything about how to call collect from a house phone, just from a payphone. After I told my grandmother what was happening, she cried, she yelled, she screamed, and she vowed that she would find a way to get me out of there. Money was tight for her, but she assured me she was going to bring me home to her in DC.

I had a long walk to get back to Chris's house. By now, it was something like 10 p.m. and after curfew—not a good combination for a teen on the streets of Chicago. The police saw me, and I was arrested. I told the police officer to call my friend, Chris, and not to call my father, but they called him anyway. Even after I told them what he had done to me, they didn't care. They still called him.

Once he arrived at the gas station—the police opted not to take me to the police station—he didn't ask where I'd been, if I was okay, who I'd been with, or any of the typical questions a parent would be expected to ask a child who hadn't been home in days. What he did do was tell me to get into the car. I got in, and that's when he punched me in the face before then delivering a verbal blow of "No one will ever believe you because I told them you always run away."

That ride was the scariest that I have ever taken. I didn't know what to think. Was he going to beat me again? Kill me and say I ran away? I just didn't know what was about to happen.

As we pulled up to the house, he told me to wait outside, then he opened the side door to the basement and told me "Get in there." He didn't feed me nor did he ask how I was but just told me to get in the basement.

So, the next morning, I left at the appointed time of 6 a.m., and instead of being gone until seven that evening or for two or three days, I never went back. I lived in abandoned buildings and made money washing dishes at a rib shack.

All I wanted was love from somebody. My aunts had their own kids and didn't need another mouth to feed, and I would cry. I needed my mother, but she was no longer here. This is when I started getting mad with God. *Why couldn't You let my mom stay so she could take care of me? Why?* This was so messed up on so many levels.

I called Dad (my adoptive father) and my aunt, begging them to come get me. They didn't, and they soon stopped taking my calls. I had no one, and it remained that way even to this day. As I got older, I got my own car and wanted to be around my family. Although they called me "brother" and "son," it never really felt like I belonged nor did their actions toward me suggest that I belonged. I couldn't go to them for help with anything. If I called, just needing advice, they would listen to my problem only to say "I don't know" or that they couldn't help me, and then they would proceed to tell everyone in the family about what I had asked for or what I needed.

I remember one time I had passed the written test for a job that I wanted so badly. The good news came when the company called me to let me know that I had been selected for the position and that the next step in the process was a background investigation and a drug test. I was elated! I was instructed to report to an address to take a drug test, and it was there that I would also pay for my background check. It was a Tuesday, and all of this needed to be done that week, by that Friday. I called my adoptive dad and asked if I could borrow $75, promising him that I would give it back as soon as received my first paycheck. Surprisingly, he told me that he did not have it, that he was sorry he could not help me, but that he wished me luck. I said, "okay," and we hung up.

Ten minutes later, my sister called me, needing $200 to make the last payment on her ticket to Jamaica. Ordinarily, I would help her, but this time I didn't have the money; so she said, "Let's call Dad." With me on three-way, she called him, and he told her, "Sure. I can help you. When do you need it?" She told him that she would meet up with him later and get it, and he said that was fine.

Once she disconnected the line with him, I told her what I had just asked of Dad and how he had told me that he couldn't help me. I was crushed. I was broken to hear my Dad rush into complete giving mode for my sister but shut me down when I went to him asking for money that I needed to get a job. I was done!!!

You see, it's the times like this that shape my views of my family. I feel like the bad kid at the party, the unpopular one who's waiting to be picked for the game only to get picked last or not at all. Parties, family get-togethers, trips, anything, and everything—I'm the last to get called, or I don't get called at all.

Did my family know I was homeless?
Yes!

Did they know my marriage was rocky, and I needed help?

Yes!

Did I call out for help many times?

Yes!

But I just didn't matter.

While writing this book, I called my biological father and asked him if he'd ever loved me. He said "yes," but his pattern of behavior still didn't change. He doesn't call me and doesn't come to see me. He doesn't even know my kids. Actually, no one does for the most part. But that's not the point. He says he loves me, but his actions do not send the same message.

So, do I feel rejected? Yes. And what will I do about it? I vowed that I will never treat my children the way I was treated. I vowed to love them in action and in deed—spend time and make the phone calls.

And although it seemed pointless to try because of all the things I had endured, I took that step anyway. I spent more time with me for me. I read the Bible even when I didn't want to. I told myself that I loved me even when I didn't feel it. I helped people even when I thought that they didn't deserve it. And I stepped out of fear to accomplish goals. I let go. I! LET! GO!!!

We all have people in our lives who profess that they love you, that they are there for you, and they've got your back. But as soon as *their* friends, family, or co-workers whom they hold dearly show up, the whole story changes. These same people treated me differently—speaking very disrespect-fully to me, giving and showing love and respect to everyone except me. What do you do when this happens? How do you act? And most of all, how do you feel?

I have been through this more times than I can count. Although people may say "you're family," you will never be, no matter how badly you may want and need that. But there is nothing like your own. I wanted a family so badly that I would insert myself into a place or a relationship where I should not be just to feel like I was almost a part of something. You know that "almost" kind of love—"almost" meaning it's not enough to register on any gauge of emotions. My own family didn't want me, didn't love me, and mistreated me so badly that I looked for family in the women I dated, in my friends, and in their families.

I had to learn to love the family God gave me even if it was from a distance. And in doing so, do you know that although my family was super jacked-up, there were two major things I learned? One, I had to love me or learn to love me. It was loving me that allowed me not to get upset or angry when family didn't show up for me, be it a special event or an emergency. Two, my family played an integral role in helping me to be forgiving. I liken this to Joseph in the Bible after he was sold into the slavery by his brothers. What did he feel at that very moment? Did he feel forgiveness toward his brothers, or was it hatred? I choose to believe that, in love, he forgave his family. It may have taken some time, but he did, in the end, forgive. So like Joseph, I also made the decision to forgive.

I don't really understand why things happen the way they do or even what the purpose of it all is. But from where I'm standing, I *do* understand that it is really offensive, disappointing, and tragic, and no person should ever be made to feel the way I have been made to feel for as many years as I've had to feel this way. I have to wonder … Did I do something to cause the family to set me aside, to cause the neglect? If so, then I want to take this opportunity to apologize.

When they became teens, I called my sons, Xavier and Royce, and had a long, hard talk with them about me not really being there for them and how my upbringing caused me to just not know how to care for them. I could be a father, but it was from a distance. I could give them words of encouragement and help them through whatever they were going through, but I wasn't physically there; and I apologized for it. I couldn't be there because I didn't know *how* to be there. I was never taught. I tried. I really did, but I had so many demons to deal with, so many issues, so many more downs than ups. I've been homeless too many times; I've been without all my life. I didn't have anything to give them. I failed in being a father to them and their siblings. I felt so bad, and then my son, Xavier, said that he understood. Royce said he knew, and they both had forgiven me a long time ago.

I cried after getting off the phone with them. I fell to my knees and refused to do anything less that try harder to be there for them. I have to fix the relationships with my children. It's not fair that my youngest son and the twins have all of me, and none of my other children got that. If I could go back and change things, I would in a heartbeat! I no longer wanted to live in or be in that place of brokenness. SO, I GOT UP!

It's so easy to say "I forgive," however, to act in it is another story, and I was not willing to act like everything was good every time a transgressor came around me.

CHAPTER 10

The Weight Removed

Today, I feel so rich with life, love, and purpose. One day, after morning prayer and some deep reflection, I felt especially full of love and purpose and needed to write. I grabbed a pen and notebook, and I started writing a letter about the pain and the hurt from the ones who got away with the most heinous of crimes—murder and the mistreatment of a child. I understood that for me to grow to the level of the man that I was put here to be, I had to release and forgive in all areas of my life.

This was not an overnight revelation. This process took months and years to even want to write and explore my feelings on paper. It's so easy to say "I forgive," however, to act in it is another story, and I was not willing to act like everything was good every time a transgressor came around me. I wasn't! So, in writing this letter to the man who murdered my mom and to my biological father, this is me forgiving and letting go. WOOOOSAAAH!

Dear Leon and Russell,

I know this is sudden and out of the blue. I have never written you before, and to be on a letter together, you might be asking *"What the hell is going on?"* Well, before we get into that, let me introduce you both. Russell is my biological father, and Leon is the man who killed my mother. I put you both on this letter, for you have something in common. As you read this letter, you will understand the similarities. I will start with you, Leon.

Leon,

I really do pray that this letter releases me from you as we were connected by my mother. I love my mother. She is the beat of my heart, the holder and shaper of my world, the teacher of love, caring for me and others. She's my first love—and you took that from me. Why? I don't understand. I have been in many fucked-up relationships, looking for the love that I didn't get growing up. Even now, I long for a hug from her, a kiss, encouraging words—shit, just a basic conversation. Do you know what it feels like to grow up and everyone treats you like you're a burden? Everyone, including family, treats me like shit because they know that I didn't have anyone to protect and save me. The holidays at home were miserable. I felt sad seeing how friends' parents loved them and hearing their conversations that started with "My Mom" or "Hey, Mom."

I grew up never knowing the words "it will be okay," "you can do better," "it's all right," and "I'm so proud of you." My pain was every day, all around me. I needed that motherly love so badly that I would intrusively place myself in my friends' families, in girlfriends' families—shit—in *anybody's* family.

I was adopted, and that was a fucked-up part of my damn life. Do you know that no one will love you like your mom can and will? You selfish son of a bitch. You took peace from me and gave me hell, hardship, and constant pain. The night you killed my mother, you killed her children, too, and I hated you so much until I wanted to kill you.

Let me ask you this: How much time did it take to plan to go to her job, hide in the woods until she got off, beat her to the point she couldn't move, and then lay her in the street for a car to run over her?

I wanted to hurt you. I even found you at one point. I saw you, and God saved you. But you know what? Even while I look at this letter that I'm writing, you're not worth a thirty-three-cent bullet.

Russell,

You became my father after I came out of the foster home. I looked to you for protection, peace, love, and leadership. Leadership, not guidance. Leadership means walk with me. I needed you to teach me, to show me, to be with me, to guide me. All the other kids, including my cousins, had their dads, and I had nothing. Damn, man I'm your son. You won't even call me by my name! For the record, my name is not Buddy. My name is Mark. You should say it a couple times. It's easy and short—Mark.

I felt like it was my fault you didn't want me. Even right now—you live in the same state and are only twenty minutes from me, but you still won't call. I have tried. I have called, and you keep saying the same damn thing: "Let me call you back after I finish doing this one thing." And yet again, it's been four years. When will you be done?! Damn. You would think you would stop for your only born child. You took your wife's children and kicked me to the curb, literally. I don't wish any harm to you, but I hated you to the point that I once *did* want harm to come to you. The way you would beat me and the things you would say would kill me, then I would wake up the next day like *Shit. I should have died.* I begged for death, but it wouldn't come. Why are there people in the world like you who do so much harm to children and their families? Why? But to me, you are a piece of shit person. What kind of man does that to a child? You even let your friend beat me as if I was there for him to use to release his stress. And you let him steal my hope with every lash of the belt. He took my want to live with each stroke while I was reaching out to you only to see your evil ass wife telling you that I was not your problem.

You killed my dreams of being like you. You were my superhero. Nobody is badder than my dad. I wanted to be you. You know I'm glad I'm not. I had Rob whom I call Grand-dad because he earned it. My adoptive father did what he could. I'm not making excuses, but he was there. You did nothing for me. I hung out with good and not so good people and thugs just to get fatherly attention, and they stepped up. BUT IT WASN'T THEIR PLACE TO DO THIS.

I learned to carry a gun and hide drugs at twelve. I shot a gun and was selling drugs at thirteen. I saw people get shot, and I saw my first dead body at thirteen. Dad, that's why I ran to you when you came back. I was tired of seeing this every other day. The one thing I did have was protection—the guys would not let anything happen to us and would fight those who would look at us wrong, but your bitch-ass would beat me like I stole something from you. I never stole money. When I was hustling, when I was holding and hiding, these guys loved me and treated me like their own son. But you would beat me because the wind blew. *If it wasn't for the barbeque spot in Chicago that hid me from you and that called Grandma back in DC, you would have killed me. So, now you should see the relationship between you and Leon. You both killed my mother and me. I went through life without love and everything that my mother had for me. I am alone even now in terms of family. So, I built my own. My fiancée loves me in ways that it can only be God giving me what I didn't get growing up. God bless your mother and sisters and your brother, Vincent, for doing their best.

Thank you for being shit because out of it, a man grew. I'm not the perfect father, but I am damn sure not you. So, as I end this letter, I will say that I forgive you both for what you have done, and I mean it. I don't want a relationship with you, however, I pray no harm to you—just love and good energy.

Wow! I feel so much better! Letting go is awesome and needed. Thank you, God, for this opportunity.

*After my father threw me down the stairs into the basement and after he'd picked me up from the gas station where the police found me to only beat me again that night, when he let me out the next morning, he told me I had better come home that day or he would kill me. That was when I ran away a second time, staying in an abandoned warehouse building for several days. When I went out in search of food, I thought he saw me so I ran as fast as I could and ended up running into a restaurant—a rib shack—where I asked the lady who managed the place if she would help me. Without question, she took me into the back, gave me a drink of water, and told me I was safe. I asked her to call my Grandma who lived in DC. She did, and in the course of their conversation, my Grandma told her that she would take care of getting me home to DC and asked if the lady would help me in the meantime. The lady said she would, and she did. She fed me, and I worked there for four days, washing dishes and cleaning up. She paid me for my work and told me the money I'd earned was for me to use to get back to DC. And that's precisely what I used it for. I had someone drop me off at the Amtrak train station, and I returned to DC.

God put me in the presence of the woman who would become my everything.

CHAPTER 11

The Gift

As I opened my eyes and simultaneously took a slow, deep breath while lying in my king-sized bed, enjoying the warmth of the sunlight shining through my bedroom window, I quietly thanked God for another day. I sat up and said, "Today is going to be a momentous day," then I walked into the master bathroom to brush my teeth and wash off the residue of a great night's sleep.

I didn't know why at the time, but that day felt so different from any other day. It felt like a loving hug, a warm surprise, and an unexpected gift all in one. And it felt so good after the year I had had with losing everything I owned and having to start over again. It sucks having to return to start and not being able to pass go.

I had just ended a relationship with a woman who came into my life like a slice of birthday cake—sweet, fluffy, and caring. It all seemed so good until I took off the blinders only to realize I was standing in the middle of an eight-million-acre field filled with bright red flags. I was thinking *Damn, man! How did I miss this?!*

However, in all honesty, I know why I overlooked the flags—it was because I was having so much fun with her. It was to the point that I didn't trip too much when she would leave and be gone off the grid for a couple days. I didn't care about the stupid high school reasons she would give when I started asking where she was. I just laughed, and besides, I was chillin' with my friends, smoking cigars, and drinking. Her absence wasn't a big deal because while she was out, messing around, God put me in the presence of the woman who would become my everything.

As an engineering supervisor for a residential complex, one day, I was called to assist a young tech with restoring heat to a resident's home. As a teaching supervisor, I jumped at the opportunity to help and teach. However, when I arrived at the resident's home, the tech had left, and the heat had not been restored. It was getting late in the afternoon, the sun would set soon, and it was getting colder out by the minute.

I knocked on the door, and this beautiful light-complexioned woman who stood about five foot two answered. I said to myself *Wow. She's beautiful.* I told her I was there to fix the heat, so she let me in. I looked at her, but I didn't stare; and I never date anyone on my job, in the same neighborhood, or a friend of a friend.

I started working on the unit when I realized just how extremely cold it was in this woman's home, prompting me to ask her how long she had been without heat. Do you know she told me it had been two weeks?! *Two weeks?!! What?!!!* And it was the winter of 2018–2019, that one winter where it just snowed and snowed; it was so cold until the air stopped blowing, and you couldn't find any gusts of wind possibly hiding in the lobbies of buildings. There was just the still, wintry cold.

I found the problem—someone had incorrectly wired the unit, so I had to start from the beginning with the thermostat and wire it to the unit. All the while, the resident was bundled up, sitting in front of her computer, working like it was nothing. Or she was fakin' the funk. But after two weeks of no heat, perhaps she'd simply become accustomed to the achingly low temperatures. And not only did the bitterly cold indoor temperature get my attention, but I also noticed how quiet the place was. It was so quiet in that home until you could hear the devil whispering to someone down the street. I continued to work on the unit, mindlessly remembering the rules of the connections.

Green on green.

Blue is common.

Yellow is ...

And white goes to ...

Then bam!!!!!

We had heat!

I told the resident that I had fixed the problem and that she would soon feel the temperature warm. She smiled at me, and I could feel so much peace from her that it made me strike up a conversation that was amazing and that went on for about twenty minutes. I fought to make myself leave because I don't normally do this with clients, however, I could see myself just talking with her all night. Nonetheless, I left and went to my next heat call.

Months later, one thing led to another, and I split with the woman I had been seeing, the one who had me with my blinders on. It was the dead of summer, and I don't know who was in charge of the heat. All I know is they fell asleep and pushed the thermostat to redemption. As we would say in DC, it was hotta than a mug. On this hell-filled week of heat, the birds were flying on fire, and demons were repenting, asking for a cooler day.

I was asked to help residents by fixing any broken AC units. I said I would help, and yes, you guessed it—my second work order was my crush. I hadn't committed her address to memory, so when she opened the door looking crazy, sweaty, and just all-around hot, it was a welcome surprise. I felt an excitement come over me.

"Hey! How are you?" burst out when I opened my mouth.

I could tell she was also happy to see me, however, in the back of my mind, I couldn't help but to think she may not have necessarily been happy to see me, Mark, but that she was happy to see me, the person who would repair her AC.

As I walked in, she said, "It's good to see you again."

Believing the look on my face made it clear that the feeling was mutual, I went on to say, "Your energy is so peaceful."

She smiled and replied, "Thank you."

I went into the HVAC closet and got straight to work. Five minutes passed, and in that short amount of time, I knew I would not be able to restore the unit to working order in that one visit. The AC unit was low on freon, which had caused it to freeze, and I had to turn off the unit and wait for it to thaw before I could restore service. I told her I needed to return the next morning to finish the job. But knowing that it was going to be really hot that night, I invited her to come and sit with my friends and me around the corner until the temperature of the summer day cooled off.

With surprise in her voice, she said, "Okay. That's cool!"

The look on my face was one of delight. And then I asked, "What's your name?"

"Jen."

I was in no way looking for a relationship; in fact, it was not even on my mind. I was just happy to be her friend, to sit in her peace, and enjoy great conversation.

I returned to her home the next day to complete the AC repair. After that, weeks went by without me seeing Jen again.

Then one day, while I was sitting outside after work, smoking a cigar, grilling chicken, and listening to music playing in the background—this was my version of after-work partying that went on every day rain or shine—I looked up and saw her waving to me from across the street. I waved back with a gesture that beckoned her to come over as I walked in her direction to meet her in the middle of the street. And guess what she said! Do you know she revealed that she had been looking for me and that she was glad to have found me?!

I felt a BOOM!

It exploded in the middle of the street.

It made my heart melt just to know that she wanted me in her peace.

I told her, "This is where I am. If you want to come by, you are more than welcome."

She smiled, said "okay," walked off, and I went back to my after-work partying.

Approximately a week passed when I was sitting with my friends and this beautiful angel, Jen, walked up and said "hello." Again, I felt so much peace radiating from her that all I could do was smile. My friends were immediately accepting of her, characterizing her as being "cool." Agreeing with them, I replied with "I know. I'm going to make her a new member of our crew." My friends all approved, saying that it was a good idea.

So, every day I would grill and play music, and we would smoke cigars, have drinks, talk trash about our day, laugh, and just have a good time. This went on for weeks and months at a time, and Jen and I got to know each other. She became my best friend.

I didn't tell Jen all the details of my life like having to eat out of the trash behind Popeyes and Church's Chicken or about being raped as a child, but I told her enough. Part of the reason I didn't tell her everything was because when I told everything to others in past relationships, they would judge me so badly, forgetting the man I was in front of them in that moment, not respecting me for what I'd been through and who I'd become. I didn't divulge it all because I didn't want the same reaction from Jen. I didn't want her to judge me like others had judged me. And another reason I didn't tell her was because she would cry from the little things that I *did* tell her, so to avoid hurting her even more, I kept the rest to myself.

Our friendship eventually became more than that of a best friend; this became abundantly apparent after a cookout.

One weekend, my neighbor and I hosted a fish fry, and I provided the music by deejaying. There was a total of about fifty people, and my best friend, Jen, was there, which helped to make it an awesome day with so much fun. As the sun started to set, we cleaned up, I put away my system, and several of us went into my house to watch the movie *Soul*. As we sat on the couch together, Jen leaned on me, so I put my arm around her. Then as the temperature dropped due to the AC's cool air blasting through the vents, I got a blanket and covered the two of us with it, which caused her to not just lean on me, but now her head was lying on a pillow that rested on my lap. We continued watching the movie and I felt so much energy around us—so much so until she abruptly jumped up and left.

Trying to give her space, I didn't call, but I did immediately text her.

I had a great time. Will I see you tomorrow?

Yes. Good night.

I was a bit puzzled by all of this, but I still needed time to myself to understand the energy I felt from her. In retrospect, what was happening is we were on the precipice of crossing that line from just having a friendship, and we were moving into a new territory, a territory of a loving and intimate relationship.

A couple of days went by, and I hadn't heard from Jen nor had I seen her. There had been absolutely no communication, so I went to her apartment.

When she opened the door, I said, "Hey! How are you?"

And before I could get another word out, she said, "Look. You're an awesome man with great standards, a father who loves his children. You treat everyone with honor and respect. Your friends and co-workers respect and love you. I feel so much love from you. You treat me better than I could ever imagine. I need a man like you. I want to be married, and I don't—."

I interrupted her.

"Marry me."

Up until that moment, I didn't know that she felt the same, and quite honestly, I didn't know if I was even ready for a relationship. My initial thought was not to tell her how I felt. But it was clear. She was my everything, and I didn't want my past to hurt what I was trying to build. It was time to keep moving forward.

Again, I said, "Marry me. I want to spend the rest of my days with you."

She started to cry and said "yes," that she had been waiting for me to ask! She said she loved me, that she would never hurt me, and that it would be an honor to be with the man God had made for her. That made my heart melt.

And I can say that was the best decision I have ever made, asking her to be my wife! I have grown to love her, and the love continues to grow every day. Things are not perfect, but she's perfect for me. Thank you, God, for this gift. I prayed for all that this woman is, and God gave it to me and more. So, going through all the hardships to learn how to love, act, talk, protect, and provide was so I would be fully able and ready to love and give what I had learned to Jen. I understand now, and I thank You, Father God, for the lesson. I will marry Jen. I will pour into her all she pours out for me. She treats me in love, and I feel it every day. We are together every day, and it's heaven. I see the gift, and I thank You, God.

I finally learned that
I was worth life and
love. I was broken from
being told I was shit,
that nobody would love
me or want me, and
that I was God's reject.
I decided not to take
it anymore. I decided
I deserved better than
better. I deserved
the best!

CHAPTER 12

The Journey Continues

It took some time for me to get my shit together. I found me. I found my voice once again, and I found my worth, my peace, and my love for self. It didn't matter how hard the work was that I had to do to find me, I did it anyway. It was not a pleasant experience, and the road was rough.

I was displeased with myself most of the time, and many of the decisions that I made as a teenager—dabbling in drug sales—and as a young adult—mistreating women—were not always the best ones. But I was receiving messages from all around me that I was going to get back up on my feet. I was determined to get back to my kids and be the father they deserved to have in their lives. I was determined to have my life back. I was focused and didn't let anything get me down despite all the challenges I faced. When I look back on those years, I know that most of the pains that I went through and most of the struggles and experiences that I had were meant to prepare me for life ahead.

And the struggles came from all different directions—family members, girlfriends, and people whom I trusted and loved—there were so many struggles. And what really got to me was the name-calling. No matter what I did, I was always a liar, a cheater, or a hypocrite, and on top of that, they took me for a stupid, childish, and selfish person. This is why I stopped telling my hurt and sharing my feelings because if a person wanted to hurt me, they could by using my past, by using what I'd shared, by using my fears and my life against me.

So, I say no more!

I deserve better!

I finally learned that I was worth life and love. I was broken from being told I was shit, that nobody would love me or would want me, and that I was God's reject. I decided not to take it anymore. I decided I deserved better than better. I deserved the best!

Do you know how it feels to be accused every other day of cheating or lying, combined with justifying and deflecting? It gets rough and old really fast. And the wild thing about those experiences is that I would do all that I could to prove that I wasn't doing what I was being accused of. I worked hard to show up for my woman and do whatever it took to please her. But it seemed that I couldn't do any good or anything of value in her eyes. However, I simply chose to accept this as my reality just so I could have a relationship. I needed to be healed from my abusive past, and not until then would I attract anyone or anything different down the line.

Because I wasn't fully healed of my issues and because I was unaware that that was fueling my relationship choices, I dated women who would really treat me like crap. But that's what I was used to—the mistreatment and the abuse as a child—so it was normal for me to be accepting of harm again in my relationships as an adult. It wasn't always physical;

it was in some ways emotional and mental abuse. But I know now that abuse is abuse—no matter you dress it. The manipulative behaviors and the mean and hurtful words became so much more damaging to my mind; my self-esteem lowered to being almost non-existent. I would, in turn, become angry on the inside. I wouldn't lash out, but I would feel so helpless, stupid, worthless, and unsure of myself. These negative emotions affected me in my everyday life and at my job.

I doubted myself even in things that I knew as well as I knew the back of my hand. It got so bad that I ended up getting fired, and it was for the best because I would have eventually hurt or killed someone or myself with the mistakes I was making on the job. And you know when you lose your job, everything else follows.

I have lost my possessions so many times that I just stopped buying nice things because I didn't feel that I deserved them even though I know I did. Sometimes I would even let a woman talk me out of loving myself and having precious personal possessions. I am by no means blaming anyone, and this is not a pity party; these were my decisions to make, and I take full responsibility for my actions. They were mine and mine alone. I'm showing you where I was and what I went through to get to a place where I said enough is enough and I refused to live another year, month, week, day, or second like that.

As I think about all that I have been through, I understood it all, but I didn't like where I had to go and what I had to do—the feelings, the emotions, the memories, and the decisions—to make me a better person, man, father, and fiancé. I didn't want it to happen. I didn't want to face anything; however, I thank God for it all. My life was like this big nasty, blistering, puss-filled painful wound. Just think about it—if I can see it, smell it, and feel it, then everyone else can see and smell it, too. And the only way for it to heal is to remove the bandage, open it up, cut away the dead flesh, and wash out the bacteria. But please understand for full healing to occur, there must be a passage of time—being able to stand in a place, ready to work as the process manifests itself. Acknowledging, accepting, and taking responsibility for myself and all those actions is the uncovering of the wound. It hurts more to uncover than it does to let go, to cut and turn away. It wasn't until then that I finally stopped causing the greatest harm to myself.

I stayed in a place of anger, a place of pity, and a place of brokenness, seeing everything as my fault and my responsibility to figure out on my own. I could have gotten help from a counselor. But I didn't. I could have listened to God telling me to take all my cares to Him. But I didn't. I stayed in that dark place. However, when I started to make my way to the place called better is when I got better. It bled badly, but it was greatly needed.

I knew, in my mind, that I could be better. The only thing preventing me from reaching my end goal was the path that I needed to take. I had the conviction that I would be back to help others get their lives together, to get them back on their feet. But there is one thing that was in the way: I couldn't help others if I couldn't find a way to get out of this rut myself. So, I knew that the onus was on me to find a way to get back on my feet, get my stuff together, and find my way through the rough.

This motivation kept me going when it felt like I should quit. When it felt like I couldn't continue, when it felt like I could no longer take it anymore, I remembered all the people I would let down. I had grown to be that someone who didn't like to rely on people for anything, but I knew there were people who relied on me. There were people who I couldn't let down. I knew I must find the drive to get back to a place where I had peace, calmness, and joy back in my life.

When I was homeless with my sons, they were very young, and we were sleeping in abandoned homes in northeast Washington, DC and in the waiting area at Union Station. I washed them in a grocery store bathroom before taking them to school. My mind was super focused, so much so that I didn't care how I looked or smelled as long as I was doing for them and working toward creating a better life for us.

I reached out to a strong friend, mentor, and father fig-ure, Chaplain Gleason. He and his wife took us in and are the most caring, loving people I have been blessed to live with, and for that, if or when they call me, I drop everything and I'm going. When I told Chaplain Gleason—now Pastor Gleason—that I had to leave their home because I had enrolled in a program that would help us get our own place, the whole family was upset. I thought *God, these people love us.* And, man, they loved us for real! To have felt that love opened the door for me to not only want more but to live like them. I love them as if they are blood kin.

But I had to go.

The program afforded us a hotel room, plus I received food stamps and a little cash assistance every month. When I say I was truly grateful, I could kiss God's face as a forty-hour-a-week job just to show my gratitude and love and not get tired. This walk has humbled me, and I respect the move of God and all the blessings that have come my way.

I didn't know how to be a parent and wished I had a manual. I asked God to lead me and help me, and He did.

He provided, and I was able to take care of my sons in such a way until they didn't even know we were homeless.

My kids, my family, and my friends (not that I had too many of them) were some of the people whose messages kept repeating in my mind. The more I remembered them, the more I knew those people needed me in their lives as much as I needed them in mine. I found the energy and zeal to stay focused at the So Others Might Eat's Center for Employment Training (CET) program and graduated with a certificate in HVAC Building Maintenance/Engineering/Leadership/Management.

After I finished at CET, I got a job as a chief engineer. This is how I got my life back in place, and I was able to double-down and fast-track getting a home of my own, be with my sons, and return to normal. What I care for the most in my life are my twin sons; I got them back. They were five years of age when I got them back from my ex-wife, and now I am happy to be their father and claim my responsibility as a father in their lives. At the time of this writing, they are fifteen years old, and I see them as the constant motivation that reminds me of the daily struggles that I went through before I could get them. I got motivated more and more as I envisioned us living happily together. I wouldn't want to lose all of that again. So, at least I owe it to them to keep at the good work and continue to be a source of inspiration in their lives.

In the midst of understanding life, I came to a wall—a wall that caused a lack of what understanding is. The wall is what communication prevents, for when you have communication you have clear flow—no restrictions. But also know that this doesn't mean that understanding or communication works alone. Even after the wall is removed, there are still additional working parts that include respect, love, understanding, knowledge, family, and God. I was always told that with this, you have everything.

You will come across people who don't want to listen to you. There are people who will over-analyze and read into something that is not there. With that, you have to stand your ground, be firm, and believe in yourself. For me, standing firm meant knowing I was still worthy, that I am smart and loved and that God loved me, that I wasn't a piece of trash as others would have me to believe, that I wasn't the devil's spawn.

Sarcastic remarks from others will lead to a mental shake-up, but it's okay. Don't let it be your food of the day. We, as a people, let too much stress in, and then we let our own emotions take us out of character. At times, sarcastic comments are the emotions of the speaker, and the sarcasm can be the result of their own lack of understanding, or it could be a result of what was said striking a nerve with them. Learn to be as a stone in the open field—the wind may blow on it, around it, and against it but not through it. Things can push you around only if you let them. Congregate with fools, and you fall to the weakness of foolishness and defeat. Stand alone, and be strong.

I now have my own family—sons, daughters, and a very beautiful woman at my side. And love is the foundation of everything that I do. I know that I have been through the fire with how I grew up, and there were a lot of mean and hurtful things said and done to me on a daily basis as a child and even as an adult. But the best gift for me is to acknowledge all these things, accept them, then learn to speak life into myself.

I call it a gift because it helps me identify where change needs to be applied. I no longer let my past keep me from life's happiness. I make the decision to break the chains, to break the generational curses. I forgive those who wronged me. I forgive myself for holding on to the pain and anger for so long. I forgive. I found that through my decisions to be a better person, man, and father is when I found that people who hurt me in the past have moved on with their lives, so why am I holding on to the things that they did when they have since forgotten all about those events? Knowing this, I started to make changes for the better, and that's when I found my true life, my voice, and love for myself. So, to those who didn't lift me up, I say thank you for the situations. Thank you for aiding in my growth.

I have since returned to the CET program to speak to the different classes and to show them that there is hope and a rainbow at the end of a storm, to let them know that there is light at the end of the tunnel, to let them know that all hope is not lost. I made it, and so can they.

I was homeless off and on for five years. While I was at Central Union Mission, I spent two years in the CET program, and those years were some of the most amazing years of my life. I was able to meet new people who inspired me to be better. I knew I could be better. I knew I had a lot in me and that the world needed to see, but I didn't know how to get there. I didn't know how to navigate my way.

Thanks go to Chaplain Philip Ford, Don Tate, Pastor David Surles, Emily Price, Ivan Laney, Karla Nelson, and many other friends who gave me the courage to pursue my dreams. I wouldn't have been able to do it without them. And after experiencing the support and protection of masons on multiple occasions throughout my journey, I was honored to become one myself. I also began professionally speaking full-time at the company I launched, Still Be Greater, and I plan to impact as many lives as possible.

Epilogue:
They Saved My Life

I've sat back and thanked God over and over again for my children. I always say that if it wasn't for them, I would be dead or in prison due to how I was living. Anger has the power to push a person to make all kinds of changes in their life. However, when used improperly, all manner of negativity will show up. Yes, I was homeless and gave up on myself for a time, but deep down inside, the drive to care for my children was more than the weight of pity and shame. It was when I decided to be better, to have better, to do better—this was when all blessings fell into my corner. The whole game changed. It was like I was shot with a superhero power beam. I only wanted to do what had to be done to get back to my children.

While I love all eight of my children—three daughters and five sons—it was the four youngest, my two youngest daughters born in 2005 and 2006 and my twin sons who were born in 2007, that I really needed to get to. To make that happen, it meant going back to school to learn a trade and having a skill that would position me to make lots of money. I had had careers in the past—I'd been a Multi-Skilled Technician/Trauma Specialist at a hospital, I'd worked on a fugitive task force, and I had even worked for a bondsman before working as a brand marketer. I needed to rebuild. I needed an apartment, a vehicle, and peace of mind. Once I achieved those goals, I knew that life would be so awesome for us, however, it would take time. I had to deal with the residuals of the past.

I stayed in the Word. This was all I had, and God made a way for me. I recognize some people are not believers and may think the Bible is not real. But after all I've been through and God showing up to make things better at different and difficult times of my life, HE'S REAL ENOUGH TO ME!

And at this point, I must acknowledge and honor the new relationship I have with my adoptive father. Starting in 2017, so much love developed between us, especially during my three-year walk to become a Mason. That love continues to envelope us, and we talk at least three times a week. One day, during a short but deep in-person conversation, he apologized for not protecting me from harm and for not being in my life more. I cried. We hugged. I felt so much joy.

I treat my children with love, and I try to do my best that they may have and not want. It may not have always worked out that way, but I tried and, man, I gave a damn good fight. I long to teach them more every day, kiss them, and watch them figure things out. It's amazing how smart and intelligent they are. I love that I need them more than I think they need me. Seeing the last four brings me so much joy. They are my reason to keep trying, to keep fighting for greatness. They saved my life.

Author's Note

Please understand that my walk helped me become the person that I am today. I learned that it had to happen in order for me to help others that may have gone through or who are currently going through the same situation. I pray that this book helps as many people as possible. The road for me has not stopped. With self-worth, love, respect, and God, I am ready for the next steps. I learned so much about me. Please take time to learn you. Get to know you. Love yourself and treat yourself to the power of change. You can change your story, so do it! Change who's around you. Change who you're listening to. Focus on God—He will lead you to success. I am by no means professing to be better than anyone else. I am just better than what I used to be. And I am so glad that I got a chance to tell my truth. I feel free—so free. Writing this book opened my eyes wider to greater possibilities of love, peace of mind, elevation, and a better self—a greater self. And I owe it all to you, God. THANK YOU, FATHER.

The many problems that we experience in our lives are meant to spur us to greatness. You can't let the challenges you are facing today be the end of you. When we encounter a problem, we have two options: We either let the problem define us, or we can resolve to forge ahead and find solutions to those challenges. I have decided not to let those challenges define me; I have decided to forge ahead with my life. I have decided to pick myself up and serve my life's purpose. I have promised myself not to look back. I may be dented, scratched, bent, and a little dirty, but I'm a good piece of equipment. Life broke me, and life put me back together. I know that it was God's plan that I was able to go from being homeless and, at times, having to sleep on a grate to be great.

I am strong enough to look life in the face and say never again will I have to feel down.

Never again will I have to look down on myself.

Never again will I allow myself to sink back into those holes that wanted to swallow me whole back then (even though I dug most of them by myself).

It's not that everything has been rosy and dandy since I made this transformation, but what I have decided is to make any challenges I face the steppingstones to my greatness—the portal to greater things. This is who I am right now, and I hope my story inspires you to also want a change. GET UP AND GO GET YOUR GREATER!

Getting to Your Greater Reflection Questions

Chapter 1

In chapter 1, I detail a tumultuous relationship with my second ex-wife, Kim. We simply were not good for each other. Relationships can be like that whether it's a spouse, a friend, a relative, or a coworker, and we each contribute to the energy that's produced—energy that can have compounding effects.

- Reflect on a relationship—romantic, platonic, professional, or otherwise—that was not healthy or that did not end well. What role did you play in it?

- What, if anything, could you have done differently that may have resulted in more positive circumstances?

Chapter 2

Quite a bit of my childhood is on full display in chapter 2, and very little of it is pretty. Adults are supposed to be our protectors, and any trauma caused during childhood can follow us into adulthood, making it hard to let go; but before you can move on, you must let go.

- When someone is hurt, they tend to hurt others—intentionally or otherwise. What have you learned about people who have hurt you? What have you learned about yourself that can help you grow?
- Did anyone cause you harm mentally, physically, or emotionally as a child? What successes have you had—big or small—that you can point to that will help you see how strong you were then and how strong you are now, that you did not allow that harm to completely immobilize you?

Chapter 3

Being homeless exposed me to a world about which most people have no clue, but even if you have never been homeless, you've experienced some sort of challenge—joblessness, feelings of abandonment, stressors, extreme overwhelm, or depression—that can make you want to throw up your hands in defeat.

- Have you ever wanted to give up on anything? It could be a small project or life itself. Think of at least one shining light in your life that gives you a reason to never give up on anything ever again—a person, an opportunity, a talent you have, a memory you want to relive over and over again, a destination you want to reach. Keep that light as a reminder to never ever ever give up.
- Who is someone who has shown you kindness? It doesn't matter if you remember that person's name or not or if it was a total stranger. What can you do today and every day to show someone else kindness?

Chapter 4

In chapter 4, I lend an ear to my sister although I'm in desperate need of someone to listen to and help me. Things turn around for me, though, when I then talk to my first ex-wife, Adrianna, and the next day when I stumble upon a surprise fortune. It feels so good when things turn around or when you can help someone turn things around.

- Although you may not have that person whose shoulder you can cry on, can you be that person who lends an ear or a word of encouragement to others when they need it without them having to ask you? You may be the only one to show that person any kindness or any mercy. What feeling would it bring not only to that person but also to you to show kindness where there appears to be none?

- Wake up each day and tell yourself that you know something good will happen to you that day. Start the day by saying these two words: Thank you. Will you do that? Positivity attracts positivity. And the more gratitude you have, the more you will be given.

Chapter 5

From experiencing bittersweet happiness with family to holding my own against strangers, in Chapter 5, the emotions I had were wide-ranging. Finding the silver lining is not always easy, but if you can, it can keep you from getting consumed.

- Whether you have a great relationship with family, a strained one, or otherwise, what are some moments for which you are grateful? Think of a time that they made you smile or that you made them smile. Keep that memory in your back pocket for when you need a ray of sunshine.
- In Chapter 5, I felt a great release as I fought the guys who cornered me in the shelter bathroom. But this wasn't a physical fight where I was just letting go of blows. This was a mental and an emotional fight where I was letting go of a lot of hurt. Holding on to hurt only holds you back; it does not propel you forward. What hurt do you need to confront and let go of today? What hurt will make you lighter if you turn it loose?

Chapter 6

In Chapter 6, I get a sign from God, and there is a light at the end of the tunnel. It requires a lot of shifts and a lot of change, but I was up for it. Sometimes a shift and a change are just what you need to light a fire under you.

- How does your day typically look? What's one new activity or endeavor you can add to your day that will bring you joy, lead to improvement, shine a light, or that will add positivity to your life?
- Have you ever been shown grace or provided with abundance that you didn't think you deserved? How can you return the favor and show others grace or provide abundance with zero motive or expectation? (Note abundance is not necessarily anything tangible or materialistic; it can simply mean a hug, a smile, or a kind gesture.)

Chapter 7

Take a moment and pray that God gives you what you need to keep going through the storm. Never ask to be removed from the situation because you will have to go through it at some point. Ask for strength, courage and for your eyes to be opened that you may receive the benefit of the lesson—the benefit that may not be immediately clear to you. If you feel misunderstood or alone, trust me—you're not alone. It might even seem like no one is answering you or is coming to help in your time of need, but they are there.

- Has anyone ever voiced a judgment call about you with which you disagreed? Maybe you were told that you're mean or rude. Objectively view that assessment. Try to see it through the other person's lens. Is there a grain of truth to it? And if so, then what can you do to be better?

- You may be in a place where you can't see the help right now because hurt or pain has your vision clouded. Think of your circumstances in their totality. For instance, did the police come when you needed them? Did the ambulance arrive just in time? Did your family member(s) show up? Wasn't there a place to hide when you needed it? And didn't you get the phone call for that job? Or money for a bill? Or food when you were hungry? Whatever your circumstance, reflect and see where God has always been there, sending you help.

Chapter 8

In Chapter 8, I constantly shift from one emotion to another both as a child and as an adult. It was so unfair. I never felt like I could just live life. It always felt like there was something I had to overcome. You may feel like that, at times, too.

- What's a challenge you need to overcome? Or what's one you can use as a motivator to help you achieve more? For me, it was my stutter and having dyslexia. What's a perceived negative about yourself that you can turn into a positive?

- What do you want so badly until you can almost taste it? Keep your sights set on it. Tell everyone you know about it—those who will cheer you on. Do everything you can to get closer to it. Think about it and work toward it every day so that you may ultimately find your way to it.

Chapter 9

We all have people in our lives who profess that they love us, that they are there for us, and that they've got our backs. But at the drop of a dime, the whole story can change. It can be hard to navigate your emotions and figure out what to do.

- Have you ever been wrongfully accused, slighted, mischaracterized, or lied to? Reflect on one instance and identify how it made you stronger. Remember "When people show you who they are, believe them the first time," per the late popular poet Maya Angelou. When people wrongfully accuse, slight, mischaracterize, or lie to you, recognize that's who they are, that that's a sign of their own character, and you cannot change them. Instead, resolve to lean on your internal strength.
- What do you need to let go of so you can feel unencumbered? Is it a person who does not pour into you, a feeling of inadequacy or failure, a limiting belief about your abilities, an idea that does not bring you joy? Let go of it today so you can be there for the people, feelings, beliefs, and ideas that lift you up.

Chapter 10

Writing can be so cathartic. It can allow you to release so many emotions. It's almost as if the pain is draining from your body, down your arm, into your hand, out of your fingertips, and into the ink of the pen as it lands on the paper in the form of your words. Even if you do not write letters as I did in Chapter 10, journaling can be an outlet that keeps those feelings from staying bottled up inside.

- What unspoken words do you need to share with someone who either built you up or who tore you down? Write a letter to that person, expressing how you feel. Say everything you've been meaning to say. Get it all out, and once you're done, you may choose to read it to them, give it to them, keep it, or destroy it. No matter what you do with it, the important part is writing the letter and celebrating the support you received from that person or releasing yourself from the hurt and the pain inflicted on you by that person. Write that letter today.

- Who is someone you need to forgive? And remember to forgive is not designed to free the transgressor. It's designed to free you from carrying the burden of harboring negative feelings about the person and/or the transgression(s). Who is someone you need to forgive and/or let go from your life? From what do you need to free yourself so you are no longer weighed down? And by forgiving and freeing yourself, what will you gain in return?

Chapter 11

It can be hard to see the obvious. All the time, we turn blind eyes and deaf ears to what we know for sure is not good for us. Realize when it's time to remove your blinders.

- What red flags are in front of you? Who or what is showing you all the signs that you keep ignoring, turning a blind eye and a deaf ear to? Who or what do you need to remove from your life, or from what do you need to remove yourself?
- What is already in your midst that can give you hope? What places and people make you happy? Spend more time there and with them than in other spaces and with other people.

Chapter 12

It's a wonderful feeling to be on the receiving end of kindness, but you cannot allow yourself to get too comfortable. In Chapter 12, I discuss the goodness of a chaplain and his wife and how much I love them but also how much I had to take leave of their home so I could do better. Sometimes you have to leave a place—even when you really don't want to—in order to continue to learn, grow, and live.

- Are you in a space that you need to move away from so you can move into an even better space? What is it, and what is the first step you need to take to get into that better space?
- What is your source of inspiration? What keeps you going? What makes you want to go get your greater?